The Political Economy of Korea–United States Cooperation

C. FRED BERGSTEN
IL SAKONG
Editors

The Political Economy of Korea–United States Cooperation

Institute for International Economics
Washington, DC
Institute for Global Economics
Seoul, Korea
February 1995

C. Fred Bergsten is *Director* of the Institute for International Economics. He was Assistant Secretary for International Affairs of the US Treasury (1977–81); Assistant for International Economic Affairs to the National Security Council (1969–71); and a Senior Fellow at the Brookings Institution (1972–76), the Carnegie Endowment for International Peace (1981), and the Council on Foreign Relations (1967–68). He is the author/editor of 22 books on a wide range of international economic issues including *Reconcilable Differences? United States-Japan Economic Conflict* with Marcus Noland (1993), *Pacific Dynamism and the International Economic System* with Marcus Noland (1993), *America in the World Economy: A Strategy for the 1990s* (1988), *Trade Policy in the 1980s* with William Cline (1984), *American Multinationals and American Interests* (1978), *The Dilemmas of the Dollar* (1976), and *World Politics and International Economics* (1975).

Il SaKong, *Visiting Fellow* (1991–92), is *Chairman* of the Institute for Global Economics in Seoul. He was formerly Minister of Finance (1987–88) and Senior Secretary to the President for Economic Affairs (1983–87) of the Republic of Korea. He is the author of numerous books on Korean economic development, including *Korea in the World Economy* (1993).

INSTITUTE FOR INTERNATIONAL ECONOMICS
11 Dupont Circle, NW
Washington, DC 20036-1207
(202) 328-9000   FAX: (202) 328-0900

C. Fred Bergsten, *Director*
Christine F. Lowry, *Director of Publications*

Cover design by Michelle M. Fleitz
Typesetting by Alpha Technologies/mps
Printing by Automated Graphic Systems

Printed in the United States of America
97 96 95   5 4 3 2 1

**Library of Congress
Cataloging-in-Publication Data**

The political economy of Korea-United States cooperation / C. Fred Bergsten, Il SaKong, editors.
    p. cm.
    Includes bibliographical references.

1. Korea (South)—Foreign economic relations—United States. 2. United States—Foreign economic relations—United States. I. Bergsten, C. Fred, 1941– . II. SaKong, Il.
HF1602.5.Z4U667 1995
337.5195073—dc20

ISBN 0-88132-213-X

94-46843
CIP

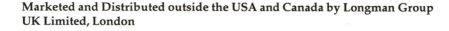

Marketed and Distributed outside the USA and Canada by Longman Group UK Limited, London

The views expressed in this publication are those of the authors. This publication is part of the overall program of the Institute, as endorsed by its Board of Directors, but does not necessarily reflect the views of individual members of the Board or the Advisory Committee.

Contents

Preface

Economic relations between the United States and Korea are of central importance for both countries. The United States has always been important to Korea but the converse is now increasingly true as well. Korea has become one of the fifteen largest economies and trading countries in the world. It has been one of the fastest growing economies for three decades and will shortly join the Organization for Economic Cooperation and Development (OECD), symbolizing its transition from a developing to an industrial country.

The Institute has thus devoted considerable attention to Korea, and its increasing importance to the world economy as well as to the United States, for some time. We analyzed its international economic position in *Adjusting to Success: Balance of Payments Policy in the East Asian NICs* in 1987 and published a compendium on *Economic Relations Between the United States and Korea: Conflict or Cooperation?* in 1989. More recently, we have published two studies of the Korean economy by leading scholars and former top policymakers from that country: *Korea in the World Economy* by Il SaKong in January 1993 and *The Dynamics of Korean Economic Development* by Soon Cho in March 1994.

The current volume derives from the first meeting of the Korea-United States 21st Century Council, a new forum launched in early 1994 to bring together top officials, private sector leaders and policy-oriented researchers in the two countries. Its purpose is to discuss both bilateral issues between the United States and Korea and their interaction on regional and global matters. The latter, including such topics as the Uruguay Round in the GATT and the Asia-Pacific Economic Cooperation (APEC) forum—are of increasing importance to the overall relationship between the United

States and Korea. We therefore organized the initial meeting of the Council and this book in three parts that present American and Korean perspectives on the bilateral, regional and global components of the relationship.

We are particularly appreciative of the strong support for the new Council by the governments of the two countries. Secretary of State Warren Christopher, United States Trade Representative Mickey Kantor, Chair of the Council of Economic Advisers Laura Tyson, Assistant Secretaries of State Winston Lord and Dan Tarullo, and Senator Paul Simon addressed the group from the American side. Foreign Minister Sung-Joo Han, Assistant Minister for Economic Affairs Joun Yung Sun, Assistant Minister for International Financial Affairs Chang Yuel Lim, Secretary to the President for Economic Affairs Choong Soo Kim and National Assembly Members Soon Sung Cho, Dai Chul Chyung, Chung-Soo Park, Woong-Bae Rha and Hak-Kyu Sohn traveled to Washington from Seoul for the session. The Council will meet again in February 1995 and we look forward to its playing an important continuing role in building better understanding of, and constructive responses to, the very broad spectrum of economic policy issues that the two countries face across their relationship.

The Council and this book are collaborative projects of the Institute for International Economics and the Institute for Global Economics in Korea. The Institute for International Economics is a private nonprofit institution for the study and discussion of international economic policy. Its purpose is to analyze important issues in that area and to develop and communicate practical new approaches for dealing with them. The Institute is completely nonpartisan.

The Institute is funded largely by philanthropic foundations. Major institutional grants are now being received from the German Marshall Fund of the United States, which created the Institute with a generous commitment of funds in 1981, and from the Ford Foundation, the William M. Keck, Jr. Foundation, the Korea Foundation, the Andrew Mellon Foundation, the C. V. Starr Foundation, and the United States–Japan Foundation. A number of other foundations and private corporations also contribute to the highly diversified financial resources of the Institute. About 12 percent of the Institute's resources in our latest fiscal year were provided by contributors outside the United States, including about 5 percent from Japan.

The Board of Directors bears overall responsibility for the Institute and gives general guidance and approval to its research program—including identification of topics that are likely to become important to international economic policymakers over the medium run (generally, one to three years), and which thus should be addressed by the Institute. The Director, working closely with the staff and outside Advisory Committee, is responsible for the development of particular projects and makes the final decision to publish an individual study.

The Institute for Global Economics is based in Seoul, Korea. It is a private, nonprofit institution that was established with two basic objectives. The first is to provide a forum for both Korean and international leaders in academia, government, business, and journalism to discuss international issues of common interest and Korea's role in the world community. The second objective is to conduct global issue-oriented research to (1) suggest alternative strategies and policies for both the Korean government and business firms to adapt to the rapidly changing international economic and technological environment, and (2) to draw attention to worldwide issues.

The Institute for Global Economics is financed by annual donations by private corporations and membership fees from business corporations as well as individuals. In addition, several of the Institute's projects are funded by public foundations. The Korea-United States 21st Century Council is partially supported by the Korea Foundation, which took the initiative in proposing the project.

IL SAKONG   C. FRED BERGSTEN
Chairman   Director
Institute for Global Economics   Institute for International Economics
                                                        January 1995

I

OVERVIEW

1

Introduction

C. FRED BERGSTEN AND IL SAKONG

The end of the Cold War and rapid technological advancements in recent years have led to two major world developments. The first is the acceleration of economic globalization. Globalization, in turn, has led to deeper economic integration among nations. Second, economics have come to dominate international relations, as countries shift their foreign policy priorities from security to economic issues. Both of these developments have resulted in far more intense competition among firms in the world market. In order to survive in this more competitive environment, firms are forming strategic alliances across national borders.

In this era of globalization and borderless economies, countries must reexamine their relationships with each other. In this context, Korean-US bilateral relations have become more critical than ever. The United States remains Korea's most valuable partner in all areas. Also, Korea's importance to the United States has risen considerably, particularly with the emergence of the Asia-Pacific region as a major global economic force.

Against this background, the Institute for Global Economics in Seoul and the Institute for International Economics co-hosted the first meeting of the Korea-US Twenty-First Century Council in Washington. Leading businessmen, government officials, scholars, and politicians from both countries participated. In order to systematically address the myriad issues involved, the meeting was organized to discuss the Korean-US relationship in its regional and global as well as bilateral contexts.

On a bilateral level, the Council considered how the end of the superpower military conflict will affect the overall relationship between Korea

C. Fred Bergsten is director of the Institute for International Economics, Washington. Il SaKong is chairman of the Institute for Global Economics, Seoul.

and the United States. Of particular interest was the future bilateral economic agenda. Questions were raised regarding possible sources of trade tensions, especially what new problems the bilateral relationship would face as Korea enters the ranks of industrialized nations. In this regard, participants discussed new opportunities for bilateral economic cooperation, such as forging US-Korean industrial alliances. The Council also considered how Korea and the United States might work together in seeking improved market access to Japan.

At the regional level, the Council posed the question of whether, with the end of the Cold War, the United States and Korea have common or conflicting goals in their relations with other countries in the Asia-Pacific region. For example, do they share the goal of "containing" China militarily while simultaneously encouraging Chinese economic development and democratization? How should they deal with Japan's growing economic and political impact in the region?

The Council also explored ways that Korea and the United States could promote regional economic cooperation, particularly in trade and investment. In doing so, it addressed the important question of whether there are conflicts or complementarities between regional and global trade liberalization, specifically with the conclusion of the Uruguay Round of trade negotiations and such regional initiatives as the Asia Pacific Economic Cooperation (APEC) forum and the North American Free Trade Agreement (NAFTA) in mind.

On a global level, the Council focused on how the end of the Cold War has affected each country's global economic, security, and foreign policy positions and objectives. The Council tried to identify the global goals that the two countries are likely to share in the post–Cold War environment and considered ways the countries could work together more effectively on global issues of common concern.

The Presentations

In his keynote address, Korean Foreign Minister Sung-Joo Han first noted the immense and rapid metamorphoses that took place in East Asia over the last few decades, with Korea at the center of this change. With the current evolution in the Western world, characterized by the emergence of the United States as the lone superpower following the end of the Cold War, a new chapter is unfolding for the East-West relationship. The main challenge today is how to deal with the weakened but necessary US presence in the Asia-Pacific region.

Minister Han suggests two ways to meet this challenge. The first is to put in place mechanisms for multilateral cooperation in the Asia Pacific—security and/or economic. The establishment of such mechanisms would ensure continued US involvement in the region. The minister suggested that one concrete way to begin that process would be to establish a NAFTA–East Asia linkage.

Second, the United States should play the role of a "balancer" in the region. The active involvement of the United States as the linchpin in a four-power configuration would ensure peace and security in the region. The United States must recognize that such an involvement, not isolationism, is in its national interest. The strength of the future Korean-US relationship will be the central determinant in bringing about these goals.

Kihwan Kim proposes that, in view of the fact that Korean-US relations are largely a by-product of the Cold War, the time has come to review the relationship and potential changes in it more systematically. He identifies four major issues that ought to be addressed. The first is the need to end the Cold War on the Korean peninsula, which in turn involves two questions: how to deal with North Korea's nuclear problem and how to finance reunification. With regard to the first, Kim counsels patience as the most realistic and practical approach. For the second, he proposes an international study group involving the World Bank.

The second major issue has to do with Korea's powerful neighbors. Continued peace and stability require an effective institutional arrangement. To this end, the current Korean-US bilateral arrangement could be expanded to become a multilateral alliance that involves Korea's neighbors.

The third major issue is the question of how best to exploit the economic dynamism of the Asia-Pacific region. The US effort to achieve this goal through APEC is commendable. A better approach, however, might be to expand NAFTA westward to include Korea. This could start a bandwagon effect that would eventually lead to a regionwide free trade area.

The final issue is the need to minimize frictions in the bilateral economic relationship between Korea and the United States. The types of trade disputes prevalent during the 1980s are unlikely to reemerge because the source of those frictions—a mismatch of macroeconomic policies of the two countries—has largely disappeared. However, many new forms of friction will arise due to systemic differences between the two economies. Accordingly, the focus of future Korean-US economic cooperation should be how to make the two economies more compatible.

Professor Lawrence Krause argues that the end of the Cold War and rapid technological advances have reinforced the need to forge a close industrial alliance between Korea and the United States as well as to strengthen their already successful military alliance. In the uncertain years ahead, the interests of the two countries are likely to remain highly compatible: Korea is very much in need of US technological partnership while Korea's manufacturing edge and strategic location would serve US companies well in their effort to exploit the dynamism of the Asia-Pacific region.

In pursuing such a course, however, both Korea and the United States must make fundamental changes. Korea must keep in mind that technological independence is impossible and that attempts to achieve such a goal would have the opposite effect, driving away potential technology transfers. If a closer industrial alliance is to be formed between Korea and the United States, Korea must create a proper business environment and work to both overcome its long-standing mistrust of foreigners and recognize that interdependence is the key to technological progress. After decades of heavy government involvement in the economy, Korea also needs to adopt a more hands-off policy, particularly in the area of finance. On the other hand, the US government needs to expand its involvement in running the nation's economy to enhance its competitiveness.

Noting the heightened priority of economics over security issues in recent years, Rudiger Dornbusch is critical of the United States' lack of a functioning Asia policy. He calls for a more active partnership between Korea and the United States in meeting the new challenges in Asia, a region that is emerging as the center of the world.

Dornbusch argues that one potentially productive way to solidify the partnership is for Korea to make the opening move to enter into a free trade agreement with the United States. Such a move would prompt others to do the same, with NAFTA serving as a blueprint for a regionwide free trade agreement under APEC. A closer partnership between Korea and the United States would also go far toward resolving many remaining regional problems. In particular, the two countries would be natural partners in opening Japan's markets, in dealing with the emergence of China, and in exploring business opportunities in Siberia.

Soogil Young observes that the hub-and-spoke pattern of trans-Pacific interdependence that existed until the early 1980s—with the United States as the hub and East Asian countries as the spokes—has been replaced by a mosaic pattern of Asia-Pacific interdependence, due in large measure to market-driven regional integration in East Asia. While East Asia's dependence on the US market has thus diminished, trade disputes between the United States and East Asia have increased, and tensions are likely to worsen.

To deal with this problem, Korea and the United States must work together to initiate a new round of trade negotiations with a particular emphasis on investment liberalization and harmonization of national policies. Forming an Asia-Pacific free trade area may not be feasible, in view of the reluctance of some of the important players in the region and may in fact be counterproductive, as it could end up creating two trading blocs in the region. In this respect, Korea should not join NAFTA unless it is clear that Korea's entry will lead to the expansion of NAFTA to the whole region and a renewed hub-and-spoke system does not result. A key principle is that Korean-US cooperation to promote free trade in the Asia Pacific must be on a regionwide rather than a bilateral basis.

Comparing the geopolitical and economic goals of Korea and the United States in the post–Cold War era, Ambassador Kyung Won Kim finds that the two countries share important strategic interests despite the dissolution of the glue that anticommunism provided. One critical area where the interests of the two countries coincide is in their need to maintain a balance of power in East Asia. For Korea, maintaining a security equilibrium is a matter of survival, and for the United States it is vital to protecting its leadership position. The key task for statesmen is effective policy coordination that would best serve the common goals and interests of the two countries. In the area of economics, the United States needs to rethink its current approach toward trade, which involves the simultaneous use of bilateral, regional, and multilateral channels of discussion. Rather than reacting to events as they unfold, the United States would do well to formulate a "coherent architectural blueprint" that clearly defines its goals and interests.

Robert Zoellick also compares the positions and policy objectives of Korea and the United States in the post–Cold War era. Identifying a specific agenda for cooperation, Zoellick makes explicit suggestions for dealing with North Korea, for improving relations with Korea's powerful neighbors, and for furthering APEC and other regional schemes.

In this vein, the task is to ensure that the emerging economic-security-political structure—or architecture in Zoellick's terminology—remains open to new partners. An important example is NAFTA, which could provide the basis for regional integration under APEC. As for Korea, one of its most critical tasks is to develop a proper understanding of the country's place in the world; the Korean public needs to recognize that the country's rising strength carries with it regional and global responsibilities. To this end, it must urgently dispel the mercantilist atmosphere that has created a negative international image for Korea today.

The Discussions

The discussions that followed the presentations of the papers involved Korean and US representatives from both the public and private sectors as well as scholars. These discussions were highly candid and lively and covered a wide range of topics that can be divided into three broad categories: bilateral, regional, and global.

On the bilateral level, a spirited debate took place on Korea's investment climate. While recognizing that some progress has been made with respect to foreign investment, many US discussants felt that Korea remains one of the most difficult of the East Asian countries in which to invest and do business.

The response from the Korean participants was mixed. Some readily acknowledged that the problem remains serious. Others were somewhat resentful, suggesting that only American investors have difficulties in Korea, while those from Europe and Japan have been doing well. This observation was in turn rejected by the American participants as unfounded. Pointing out that most of the difficulties facing foreign businesses in Korea are shared by Korean firms as well, a few discussants suggested establishing some mechanism for cooperative endeavors—for example, a coalition of businesses—to deal with regulatory problems in Korea. Despite the divided opinion, discussants were mostly optimistic about the prospects for improving the Korean investment climate, given the current administration's commitment to reform and the positive attitude toward internationalization.

On the regional level, the issue that received the most attention was the suggestion that Korea join NAFTA. By and large, the discussants were skeptical of the viability of Korea's entry in the near future, with some even questioning its desirability.

The main reason for the skepticism is that it may be politically infeasible for both Korea and the United States. Some pointed to such practical problems as the expiration of the US administration's fast-track authority, which would make bilateral negotiations on free trade agreements extremely difficult (if not impossible). More generally, many discussants shared the feeling that, after the difficulty in passing NAFTA in 1993, there is simply not enough political will left in US political circles to extend liberalization to other countries such as Korea.

For Korea, agriculture remains a major problem. The limited level of market opening in this area has come at great political cost, and the further opening that entry into NAFTA would require would be nearly impossible. At least one US discussant noted that the agricultural issue has been exaggerated, however, pointing out that important restrictions remain between the United States and Mexico in this area.

On the global level, the focus of discussion was US leadership in the post–Cold War era. Many discussants voiced concern over the relative decline of US leadership since the collapse of the Soviet Union and over the rising influence of China in the Asia Pacific. The discussion went on to ask whether the United States, in the process, has become less generous toward its friends.

Particularly worrisome for many discussants was the response of the United States in the changing world economic environment: its adoption of a mixed strategy of unilateral, regional, and multilateral approaches to trade with an increasing emphasis on "aggressive unilateralism." While not directly challenging these observations, a number of US discussants pointed to one important and consistent feature of US trade policy: an emphasis on opening markets for US products rather than closing US markets to foreign products.

The first meeting of the Council closed with unanimous agreement that it had been extremely valuable for the participants from both countries. It was decided to meet again early in 1995 and to continue the sessions on a regular basis. All agreed on the critical importance of the Korean-US relationship for both countries and thus on the merits of the Council.

2

Korea and the United States in the 21st Century

SUNG-JOO HAN

The creation of the Korea-US Twenty-First Century Council is very timely and in some sense overdue: timely because the Korea-US relationship has arrived at such a stage that private input is critical for further progress, and overdue because Korea already has bilateral forums for the 21st century with several other countries.

Time, they say, seems to have been condensed in East Asia during the last several decades. Indeed, changes in the region have been exciting. The metamorphoses in the region have created nations that are almost beyond recognition. It is as if these countries are trying to catch up with the achievements made by the Western world during the centuries of their long and dormant history. As a matter of fact, what happened in the last several hundred years in Europe seems to be taking place within a span of several decades in East Asia. Industrial revolution, social reforms, political upheavals—all these are taking place simultaneously at a breathtaking pace.

Korea's case has often been cited as the prime example of this phenomenon. From a state of war and abject poverty until only several decades ago, Korea has emerged as a democratic country ranking 15th in GNP and 12th in trade among the 180 or more countries in the world.

Korea is participating in UN peacekeeping operations. Its contribution to the UN fund is ranked 21st. In the promotion of human rights, Korea has been transformed from a burden to an asset. With all these changes going on, Korea has come to the point of joining the Organization for

Sung-Joo Han is minister of foreign affairs of the Republic of Korea. He gave this address 18 February 1994.

Economic Cooperation and Development and pursuing nonpermanent membership in the UN Security Council.

Korea is in search of a new role. Its foreign policy can no longer be a hostage to its national division. It is time for Korea to reach out to the world and the future. At the threshold of the 21st century, which is increasingly referred to as the Asia-Pacific Era, this is indeed a defining moment for Korea.

The United States and East Asia:
A Changing Relationship

On the other side of the Pacific, we are witnessing an evolution that is no less significant. The United States led the West through the formidable challenges of the Cold War. Superpower rivalry is now over, a rivalry that had threatened the world with nuclear apocalypse. Yet with the end of the Cold War, the internal cohesion of the two camps has also been dissolved.

The expected rallying of the world around liberal democracy and market economy has proved rather insufficient in the face of regional and religious conflicts. Is the world losing a historic opportunity? Or is this simply the usual way in which history unfolds? Faced with these questions, the United States, as the world's lone superpower, is in search of a new role. This is a defining moment for the United States as well as for Korea.

Especially in its relationship with East Asia, Washington is facing a substantive adjustment. The remarkable progress achieved by the East Asian countries is propelling them to the center stage of the next act—the 21st century.

At the outset of the Cold War, East Asia accounted for less than one-tenth of the world's economic output. At the end of the Cold War, its share had increased to nearly one-fourth. East Asia, with Europe and North America, has already become one of the three major economic centers of the world. The economic weight of East Asia is expected to grow well into the 21st century.

Some say that the change in the US position on the world scene represents the beginning of the absolute decline of US power. Yet a close look shows that the so-called decline is only a relative one.

US economic power has remained constant since the late 1960s. Its military prowess is unchallenged, all the more so now that the Soviet Union is nonexistent. For a considerable period, the United States will remain the most powerful country in the world in the military-strategic realm as well as in the economic and technological fields.

It is critical for Korea, as well as other nations in East Asia, to correctly understand the change in the US position in the world and its significance.

The rise of East Asian countries—in other words, the relative decline of the United States—implies a decrease in the latter's presence in the region.

Yet the region is in need of a continued US presence. In short, how to deal with the weakened US presence in the region and the necessity of its continued presence is the single most important issue facing the countries of the Asia Pacific.

Korea's New Diplomacy

The US presence is all the more vital to Korea, since Seoul's diplomatic history of the last half a century revolved around its bilateral relations with Washington. In retrospect, the history of Korea's international relations was dominated by its relationship with China up until the 19th century, Japan in the first half of this century, and the United States during the Cold War.

The reason for this one power–oriented diplomacy came mainly from two factors: the weakness of Korea and the international order of crude "power politics." But fundamentals have been changing, affecting both factors.

First, Korea is now much more developed and stronger than it has ever been. By the 21st century, its national division will have been overcome either through unification or through a workable, peaceful coexistence. Unified or combined, Korea will be among the top 10 countries in the world—a power to be reckoned with in every respect.

Second, the world, despite all its defects, has become much more democratic and interdependent. One consequence of the growing interdependence among nations has been the globalization of issues. Balance of power and geopolitical interests will certainly continue to count, yet cooperation based on interdependence will become more relevant in international relations.

The change in Korea's international status and in the nature of the international order will necessarily alter Korea's relationship with other powers in the region and the world. Mindful of these historic changes, Korea enunciated its New Diplomacy last May featuring five fundamentals: globalism, diversification, multidimensionalism, regional cooperation, and future orientation.

- Through globalism, Korea will reach out to the world. More attention will be paid to such universal values as freedom, justice, peace, and welfare. Korea will take an active part in international efforts to tackle such global issues as peace and security, disarmament and arms control, eradication of poverty, and protection of the environment.

- Diversification will allow Korea a wider range of policy options. While maintaining and improving its relations with the United States and other traditional allies, Korea will expand its diplomatic horizons beyond the "four powers" to encompass the Asia Pacific and the world.

- Multidimensionalism will enable Korea to expand from security-dominated diplomacy to a multifaceted approach encompassing economics, environment, and culture. The World Trade Organization, the "Green Round," and the harmonization of Eastern and Western civilizations are among the important agenda items of Korea's New Diplomacy.

- Through regional cooperation, Korea intends to focus on Northeast Asian security cooperation, Asia-Pacific security dialogue, and multilateral economic mechanisms in the region, the Asia Pacific Economic Cooperation (APEC) forum being the most important one. Connecting different forces that will shape the regional order is one of the primary objectives.

- Future orientation is primarily related to the reunification of Korea. This implies a strategic effort to lead Pyongyang from isolation to engagement. Three elements will be taken into account: management of the division, achievement of reunification, and preparation for the postunification era.

Korea's new and ambitious foreign policy vision can be successful only if anchored securely to Korean-US relations. The United States is Korea's foremost security ally and largest trading partner, and it shares with Korea a common belief in liberal democracy. The Korean-US relationship can increasingly be labeled as a partnership.

A newly defined partnership between Korea and the United States goes well beyond their bilateral relationship, especially in the following two domains: the promotion of multilateral cooperation in the Asia Pacific and the enhancement of the balancing role of the United States in the region.

Multilateral Cooperation

The Asia Pacific has a unique role in the quest for peace and prosperity in the 21st century. This region now accounts for about half of the world's economic output, and its share is expected to grow. Consequently, what happens in the region will set the trends for the rest of the world.

The region, however, is in crucial need of multilateral mechanisms. These are essential to coping with the prevailing new reality—that is, a growing interdependence among nations. East Asia in particular is lagging behind in this regard. Several reasons can be identified: state-first ideology, the lack of experience and history of intraregional integration, and huge differences in size and power among nations of the region.

Yet multilateral mechanisms seem to be the only answer for dealing with the conflicting demands for the reduction of American presence and for its continued presence. Hence, there is a necessity to promote a multilateral framework, particularly one involving the United States. This may help strengthen the US commitment to the region, guaranteeing continued American presence.

"Nature abhors a vacuum" and "weakness invites aggression" are time-honored precepts of international relations that have relevance even today. Theoretically, the power vacuum left behind by the reduced US presence could be filled by Japan or China. Yet neither appears prepared to do so, and the rest of the Asian countries do not want to fill it. Such an attempt would cause great uncertainty in East Asia and raise serious qualms among most nations in the region.

America's network of bilateral alliances remains the backbone of Asia-Pacific security. A multilateral mechanism would supplement but not supplant it. Ordinarily, multilateral mechanisms led by great powers invite suspicion from other countries. Consequently, medium powers such as Korea and the countries of the Association of Southeast Asian Nations (ASEAN) are in a better position to initiate these arrangements.

On the economic front, Australia and Korea have in fact been instrumental in the creation of APEC. In security affairs, ASEAN took initiatives for regional security dialogue such as the ASEAN Regional Forum (ARF), building upon the ASEAN–Post Ministerial Conference experience. Korea for its part would like to see the establishment of a multilateral framework for security cooperation in the Northeast Asian subregion.

The economic order draws our particular attention, as aptly illustrated by the main topics of this conference. In the Asia Pacific, APEC, the North American Free Trade Agreement (NAFTA), the ASEAN Free Trade Agreement (AFTA), and the East Asian Economic Caucus (EAEC) are some of the forces and concepts shaping the regional economic order. The interplay of these forces will fix the rudiments of the Pacific economic order of the 21st century.

Among them, NAFTA is the most advanced and for that reason appears to hold the key. Should this organization become a discriminatory arrangement or continue its regional expansion only in America, then it will discourage East Asia's efforts to remain Pacific-oriented. It may even compel them to form an economic grouping of their own. EAEC is waiting to respond to such an eventuality. An Orwellian vision of the world divided into three contending blocs may not be too far removed from a self-realizing prophecy.

What Korea and the United States can do together is to preserve and increase trans-Pacific interdependence. Three avenues are open to us; the first is strengthening the global free trade system. Toward that end, the conclusion of Uruguay Round was a very encouraging sign. Further cooperation can be made to promote the WTO regime. Second is strengthening APEC, whose very raison d'être is trans-Pacific interdependence. The third avenue is the linking of NAFTA with AFTA and the EAEC.

Korea and the United States are already engaged in the first and second endeavors. We can focus on the third in the coming years. A NAFTA–East Asia linkage calls for the institutional affiliation with NAFTA of several East Asian economies. For the time being, NAFTA offers no opportunities for special arrangements other than full membership. And it is not yet clear who the prospective members are. A strong political will as well as a good deal of creativity will be necessary to institutionalize this linkage. Yet, given the high stakes of the whole region in the emerging new economic order and given the importance of this order for the entire world economy, it will surely be a worthwhile exercise.

Once such institutionalization is in sight, those prospective East Asian members of NAFTA may try to find ways to participate in other East Asian economic groupings. This would relieve apprehensions about East Asian groups; in the same fashion, the dual memberships would dissipate whatever misgivings East Asia might have about NAFTA.

This plan can be examined by Korea and the United States, along with other economies concerned. Although history constantly reminds us of the enormous power of destiny, one becomes well aware that destiny is not always determined by fate but can be forged by conscious effort. Korea and the United States together can make such efforts in order to maintain an integral and wholesome Pacific economy in the 21st century.

Promoting a US Balancing Role

The other domain of common efforts lies in the promotion of the role of the United States as "an honest broker" or "a balancer" in East Asia. This terminology reflects the shared desire of the countries of the region for US power to check any disruption of the prevailing regional order, made all the more necessary by the astonishing economic vitality of the East Asian nations.

The United States came to East Asia last century with a professed open door policy, reconfirmed by such diplomatic acts as the Bryan doctrine in 1915, the Conference of Washington in 1920, and the Stimson doctrine in 1931. At the end of World War II, Washington was committed to a new strategy of containment to check the expansion of communism. Such strategies were adopted, of course, because they protected American national interests.

Yet, one can point out a specific feature in American foreign policy: its nonthreatening nature. Numerous empires have risen and fallen in history. Most of them relied on occupation and domination, thus making themselves necessarily threatening to other nations. But American foreign policy from the beginning was heavily tinged with moralistic idealism, a unique characteristic intertwined with the founding ideology of the United States.

Its idealism has put America through difficult times, but in the long run the policies based on these ideals appear to be paying off. In East Asia in particular, most countries recognize and welcome the continued US presence as indispensable to the peace and prosperity of the region.

A nonthreatening America, along with "nonnuclear" Japan, "nonintervening" China, and "nonexpanding" Russia, will constitute the cornerstone of the peace and security of Northeast Asia, and through it of the Asia Pacific and the world. In the wake of the open door and containment policies, partnership may be the code name of US post–Cold War strategy with regard to East Asia.

The United States is called a balancer because it is the linchpin in the four-power configuration. Should Washington withdraw from Asia, as it did from the world between the two World Wars, the balance would be disturbed. In such an eventuality, there is no guarantee that Japan would remain nonnuclear, China nonintervening, and Russia nonexpanding.

The British Empire of modern Europe took advantage of its geopolitical location to claim "splendid isolation." The United Kingdom acted as a balancer in Europe, alternating between comfortable isolation and military intervention as necessary.

The Pacific and Atlantic Oceans provided the United States with enough security for it to also claim its own version of "splendid isolation" for the last two centuries. Among contemporary protagonists, the United States is the only country that still could enjoy virtual self-sufficiency, as called for by the neoisolationists.

Yet just as the United Kingdom is no longer in a position to enjoy "splendid isolation" because it is irrevocably intermeshed with continental Europe, isolationism would no longer serve US national interests; America is part of an interdependent world where all nations are organically interconnected.

For its own well-being and prosperity, the United States has keen interests in the security and economic trends of East Asia. If the United States' past lies in the Atlantic, its future lies in the Pacific—the result of the determination of the last century's pioneers to realize the American "manifest destiny," which linked North America to East Asia. Washington, which has put economic revival on top of its national agenda, is acutely aware of East Asia's importance. For the US economy, trans-Pacific trade has surpassed trans-Atlantic trade in every year since 1980. Last year, trans-Pacific trade amounted to more than $330 billion, overshadowing trans-Atlantic trade by more than 50 percent. The ratio is expected to reach 2-to-1 by the end of this century.

Such a perspective warrants us to conclude that American engagement in East Asia serves American interests. Korea can be a valuable partner in this scheme. The bilateral security alliance is the central element. This alliance system will serve not only the interests of the two countries, but also the peace and stability of the whole Northeast Asian region.

Conclusion

Academicians and theorists of international relations count the United States, Japan, China, Russia, and the European Union—commonly referred to in Korea as the "four powers"—as the protagonists of the next century. With the exception of the European Union, the interests of these powers directly converge in the Korean peninsula. Northeast Asia is at the epicenter of Asia-Pacific security.

Korea's growing power and geopolitical importance make its role in this region significant. In other words, Korea's policy options will have increasing weight and importance. Pyongyang's failure to adapt to the changing international order, as evidenced by the nuclear question, constitutes a serious problem to the Republic of Korea and to the world. The ultimate solution can come with the unification of the Korean peninsula.

To facilitate the unification process as well as to look beyond unification, Korea will focus its diplomatic efforts on helping North Korea become a participant in the world and regional order. By trying to remove the legacy of the Cold War, Korea is also contributing to the peace and stability of the Asia Pacific.

As part of this strategy, Korea will also endeavor to promote regional multilateral mechanisms. The pursuit of multilateral security in Northeast Asia, promotion of APEC, and institutional linkage with NAFTA—thus connecting it with East Asia—are some of these policy options.

Korea is now striving to internationalize its own society. Regional cooperation can be the first step to the internationalization of Korea. It also is a shortcut. Much of this internationalization can be realized in the context of the Korean-US relationship. In Korea, Westerners have commonly been called "Americans" (*miguk saram*), while in Japan they are called "foreigners" (*gaijin*).

In this respect, internationalization of Korea means harmony not only between East and West, but just as important, between Korea and the United States. Korea will serve as a medium in geographical as well as cultural aspects. It intends to play the bridging role between the East and the West, China and Japan, and between the United States and each of the major East Asian powers.

Korea has a historic task in its place at the epicenter of Asia-Pacific security. By answering this call, Korea will expand the scope of its diplomacy and greet the 21st century with hope and prosperity. In this endeavor, a Korean-US partnership is an indispensable element.

II

US-Korean Bilateral Relations

3

A Korean Perspective

KIHWAN KIM

Korean and US relations during both the 1970s and 1980s appear in retrospect to have been highly strained. In contrast, over the past few years the relationship has been relatively smooth. At the moment, the United States has no actions pending against Korea under section 301 of its trade law, no Park Tong Sung hearings are being held on Capitol Hill, and the *New York Times* and the *Washington Post* are not calling for a change in US policies toward an authoritarian government in Seoul.

Does this mean that the two countries have no serious issues to discuss and thus that the work of the US-Korea Twenty-First Century Council is superfluous? Fortunately, or perhaps unfortunately, I do not think this is the case. For one thing, we should remember that the US-Korea bilateral relationship over the past 40 years or more has been a by-product of the Cold War. Now that the Cold War has ended for much of the world, if not the Korean peninsula, the relationship is undergoing change, like it or not. It is therefore high time that we sit down together and review how this relationship has changed. Based on such a review, we should identify some key issues that should be part of the agenda for cooperation between the two countries for the remainder of this decade, if not beyond. Furthermore, we should consider how these key issues should be dealt with in our common effort for a better future.

Kihwan Kim is chairman of the Korea National Committee for Pacific Economic Cooperation and chairman of the Korea Trade Promotion Corporation; he served as secretary general of Korea's International Economic Policy Council from 1984 to 1986.

Changes Due to the End of the Cold War

One of the important changes in US-Korean relations brought about by the end of the Cold War involves the resource constraints of the two countries. During the Cold War, the United States had no option but to serve as the hegemon of the Western alliance. Securing military superiority over the Soviet Union was a necessary part of that role. It may be true that in the process the United States managed to avoid "an imperial overreach," to use Paul Kennedy's term, but there is little doubt that many of its nonmilitary needs went unmet. Now that the Soviet Union has collapsed and the United States is the only remaining military superpower, the United States is clearly in a position to reduce the level of resources committed to military uses.

One may assume that Korea, too, is now in a position where it may reduce the level of resources for military purposes. However, in the case of Korea, the extent to which it can do so should not be exaggerated. As long as serious tension still exists between the North and the South on the Korean peninsula, Korea cannot reduce defense spending without considering the consequences.

By relaxing resource constraints for the United States in particular, the end of the Cold War has affected national priorities. The United States can now afford to pay more attention to nonmilitary issues. This is most evident in the Clinton administration's adoption of domestic economy revitalization as its foremost policy priority, which it has sought to achieve largely through the increased competitiveness of US exports.

Korea, too, finds itself in a position where it must pay greater attention to increased competitiveness. For Korea, the need for increased competitiveness is perhaps even more compelling than it is for the United States simply because Korea is far more dependent on trade. But because of its continuing security concerns, Korea cannot easily shift its national priorities in favor of economic matters over military ones to the same degree as the United States can. In short, for a considerable time to come, Korea must use its resources to produce both "guns and butter."

Another important change that the end of the Cold War has brought to US-Korean relations concerns the internal politics of the respective countries, which is far more salient in Korea than in the United States. In Korea, on the whole, social groups that had prominent roles during the Cold War, such as the military, have now lost much of their political power and influence to other groups in society.

For most of the Cold War, military governments ruled Korea. As a result, the legitimacy of these governments was questioned. However, with the advent of a civilian, democratically elected government, legitimacy is no longer an issue. This, of course, has greatly contributed to political stability at home and smoother relations with countries abroad, particularly with the United States.

The end of the Cold War has drastically reduced the power and influence of radical groups in Korean society as well. Those radicals who ascribed to socialist ideology have been totally discredited in the eyes of the general public. To the extent that these radicals were both antigovernment and anti-American, their loss of credibility has not only contributed to greater internal political stability but also has paved the way for smoother relationships between Korea and other countries.

However, these improvements in Korea's internal politics, as well as in its standing abroad, have come at a high price. During the period of democratization, the country experienced tremendous increases in wages that far outstripped increases in productivity and seriously undermined Korea's international competitiveness.[1] In addition, the voice of sectoral and parochial interests has become stronger, the broad national interest has often been overridden, and protectionist sentiments have strengthened. What is more, policymaking has become more complex and time-consuming, which, among other things, has reduced Korea's ability to adapt quickly to changes in the external environment.

During the Cold War, the primary purpose of the military alliance between the United States and Korea, especially from Korea's point of view, was deterring North Korea from initiating war. This is still true to some extent. As long as tension between the North and South lasts, Koreans will value the bilateral military alliance mostly in terms of deterrence. However, as the military threat from the North diminishes, the rationale for this military alliance, and particularly the continued presence of US troops in Korea, will need to be redefined more in terms of maintaining peace and stability in Northeast Asia. As the bilateral military alliance is thus redrawn, the two countries will then need to expand their bilateral military arrangement into a multilateral arrangement.

During the Cold War, there was neither the need nor the opportunity for Korea to deal directly with its large neighbors, particularly China and Russia. With respect to Japan, Korea's heavy reliance on the United States for security and the US market for exports meant that it had no real need to court Japan in any serious way. Now that the Cold War has ended and containment is no longer a valid policy aim for the United States and its allies, Korea needs to develop more direct relations with its large neighbors. Korea's problem here is that although it has grown economically, it is still and will continue to be handicapped in terms of its bargaining power in relation to these large regional powers.

During the Cold War, the principal role for the United States in Northeast Asia was to serve as the hub of many spoke-like bilateral relations designed to contain the expansion of the Soviet Union. Now that the Soviet Union has collapsed, this role should change. However, given the

---

1. For a detailed description of this impact, see Kim (1990, 17–18).

high degree of mistrust that still prevails among major regional powers in Northeast Asia, there is a strong likelihood that, left to themselves, these regional powers would engage in a rivalry for dominant positions, as they did in the late 19th century and the early part of this century. This would no doubt create instability in the region that would be detrimental to US interests. For this reason, it makes sense for the United States to serve as a balancer between and among the major regional powers.

In addition, the United States should take advantage of the immense opportunities presented by the enormous economic dynamism of the Asia-Pacific region. In fact, increasing trade with the Asia-Pacific region is the most logical way for the United States to revitalize its economy. For one thing, US trade with the Asia-Pacific region is already larger than its trade with either North America or Europe. For another, the United States' three largest trade deficits are all with Asian economies: Japan, China, and Taiwan. What is more, the importance of US trade with the Asia-Pacific region will increase over time for the simple reason that the region is most likely to be the fastest-growing part of the world economy for at least another decade. If present trends continue, the Asia-Pacific share of world output will most likely reach nearly 30 percent by the end of the century, and the region will thus surpass North America and Europe as the world's largest economic zone (Noland 1993, 1–2).

It is important to note, however, that in exploiting the opportunities afforded by such economic dynamism, the United States is distinctly disadvantaged vis-à-vis Japan, which cemented its economic ties with developing countries in the region while the United States was preoccupied with the Soviet Union and its communist allies. In addition, the United States is geographically not part of East Asia.

Globalization of economic activity had started long before the Cold War came to an end. However, there is little doubt that the end of the Cold War has greatly accelerated this process. As a result, both the United States and Korea have come to enjoy a far greater range of choices than in the past as they seek partners for cooperation. What this means in terms of their bilateral relationship is that each country is no longer as indispensable a partner to the other as before. Because Korea and the United States often fail to appreciate this point, one feels highly disappointed when the other, long considered a special ally, acts differently from the past.

Globalization has also changed the makeup of economic transactions between or among nations. In the past, trade was the most important form of transaction between countries. Nowadays, investment is becoming just as important. In addition, the nature of the relationship between trade and investment has changed. Trade and investment are now complements rather than substitutes. This change is partly due to the growing importance of trade in services. With globalization, trade in services has become almost as important as trade in commodities. Since services cannot usually be delivered to users without direct investment, a tremendous increase in direct investment has accompanied the increase of trade in services. In addition, investment complements trade because globalization of the production process not only stimulates new investment, but also gives rise to a greater flow of trade after new investment has been completed. With the rapid increase in investment flow among countries, such issues as the removal of barriers to investment, protection of intellectual property rights, transfer pricing, and national treatment have become major sources of trade friction between countries.

In the days when globalization did not extend very far and economic linkages between countries were greatly limited, the most important barriers to trade and investment were mostly border measures. But today, the most critical barriers occur within the borders, and for the most part they stem from the structural differences of the respective economies.

In these respects, the United States and Korea are not exceptional. Thus, an interesting question is whether both Korea and the United States can remove the "new" barriers to trade and investment at a mutually satisfactory pace. This is probably more a problem for Korea than for the United States, as Korea is undergoing a number of internal political changes that are not necessarily the most conducive to rapid adjustment to a changing international environment and to free trade.

Major Issues for the Bilateral Agenda

This leads us to ask a much broader question: What does the foregoing analysis imply in terms of an agenda for bilateral cooperation for the remainder of this decade, if not beyond?

Four major issues emerge. The first of these concerns the need to end the Cold War on the Korean peninsula. The first, obvious challenge in this respect relates to North Korea's development of nuclear weapons. Both Korea and the United States share the objective of keeping the Korean peninsula nuclear-free, and both countries have a common stake in making the Non-Proliferation Treaty (NPT) effective throughout the world.

Yet it cannot be simply assumed that the two countries see eye to eye on every aspect of the nuclear issue with regard to North Korea. Although Korea wants the Korean peninsula to be a nuclear-free zone, it is less prepared than the United States to risk a possible military confrontation in order to make North Korea comply with the demands of the International Atomic Energy Agency (IAEA) for full inspection of nuclear facilities. The reason for this is simple: due to Seoul's proximity to Pyongyang, it could suffer enormous damages if Pyongyang were to retaliate against military sanctions. What makes the problem even more difficult is that North Korea would not be easily persuaded to accept the IAEA's terms unless it perceives that Korea and the United States are jointly taking a strong, common stand. Furthermore, the chances of North Korea accepting the

IAEA's demands will not be very great unless all major regional powers in Northeast Asia, including China, support any sanctions put in place. This is the dilemma facing not only the United States and Korea but all countries with an interest in the nuclear issue.

Apart from the immediate nuclear issue, and further down the road, there may come a time when Korea and the United States must work together to finance reunification. By highlighting the financial aspect, I do not mean to imply that finance is of singular importance in terms of cooperation between Korea and the United States for reunification. But there is clearly a need to call special attention to this critical issue. Judging from the German experience, the burden of financing reunification will most likely exceed the capacity of South Korea's economy, especially if reunification is not achieved peacefully and gradually.[2] In fact, there are a number of reasons to expect that the cost of Korean reunification in relative terms will be much greater than the cost of German reunification. For one thing, the size of North Korea relative to South Korea in terms of both area and population is much greater than that of East Germany relative to West Germany. The gap in per capita income between North and South Korea is much greater than that which existed between East and West Germany. Furthermore, North Korea has devoted a much larger part of its resources to military uses than East Germany ever did. As a result, the structure of the North Korean economy is far more distorted than that of East Germany at the time of reunification.[3] If Korea cannot finance reunification because of these factors, it may lead to instability on the Korean peninsula, which will affect the stability of the whole Northeast Asia region.

A second major area of concern is the need for Korea to develop and maintain good relations with its powerful neighbors. For Korea, the effort to develop and maintain good relations is very much a continuance of its efforts in 1991–92, when Korea was recognized by Russia and China and admitted to the United Nations. Unless Korea has good relations with all its neighbors, including Japan, it will be difficult for the country to survive and prosper. Further, failure on the part of Korea to have good relations with its neighbors would surely jeopardize not only Korea's own economic prosperity but also the peace and stability of the entire region. As already noted, because of Korea's inferior bargaining position vis-à-vis these countries, Korea will definitely need help from the United States. Likewise, for the United States to play an effective role as a balancer from outside the region, it will need help from an insider such as Korea. In short, in order for both countries to meet their respective objectives, they will have to work together, and in doing so, they will need an institutional

---

2. For an estimate of the costs of reunification, see Lee (1992).

3. For a fuller discussion on the greater difficulties of reunifying Korea than reunifying Germany, see Eberstadt (1992, 160–63).

arrangement that goes beyond the current bilateral arrangement, which was designed largely to meet the needs of the Cold War era.

A third area of issues has to do with the need for both Korea and the United States to work together in order to better exploit the great opportunities presented by the enormous economic dynamism of the Asia-Pacific region. It is an undeniable fact that the two countries are not in the most favorable positions to do so at the moment. Korea must find ways not only to restore its overall competitiveness, but also to offset inherent disadvantages due to its limited size, both as a country and as an economy. The United States must find ways to make up for the disadvantages due to its late start in the region and its distance from it.

A final issue relates to bilateral trade friction. As already noted, changes in domestic politics have weakened the government's ability to quickly resolve certain policy issues, particularly trade issues, just as Korea's trade problems have become more complex due to the accelerated pace of globalization. Because of these developments, the question of how the US and Korean governments can resolve trade problems expediently will continue to be prominent in the bilateral agenda.

Suggestions for Better Cooperation

With respect to the four main issue areas, what useful suggestions can one make to deal with them effectively?

The close consultations that have been carried out between the two governments on nuclear development in North Korea deserve commendation. Furthermore, the patience demonstrated by both governments has been worthwhile. However, I am concerned that, at this critical juncture, the previously exhibited patience seems to be running out. It is crucial for both countries to continue to exercise the utmost patience in dealing with North Korea in the weeks and months ahead.[4]

The grounds for this position are several. For one thing, it is true that North Korea is damaging the credibility of the NPT regime. But we should not forget that it has been doing so all along. Additional waiting for a positive signal from North Korea will do no more damage to the NPT regime than has already been done. For another, it is realistic to assume that North Korea already has a real bomb or two.[5] We should therefore be extremely careful not to provoke North Korea into making a precipitous

---

4. The course of negotiations subsequent to the conference at which this paper was presented and the recent agreement reached with North Korea in Geneva in October 1994 indicated that patience on the part of the United States has paid off. At the time the author offered this advice, however, it was not clear that the United States would remain patient. Many people in the United States, particularly in the US Congress, called for a more hard-line approach in negotiations with North Korea, but happily, the United States did not take this tack.

5. At the time this paper was presented, this view was widely shared even in Washington.

move that could do irreparable damage to itself and to others. In addition, the most probable and important motivation for the North Korean regime to possess the bomb at this moment, from their point of view, is deterrence. Thus, the regime is unlikely to use the bomb unless it feels that its survival is seriously threatened by an external power. Furthermore, the experience of the Soviet Union should indicate that, in the long run, the viability of North Korea will not depend on whether it owns a bomb. What is more, if the world tolerates the Commonwealth of Independent States' safeguarding their nuclear weapons, there is no reason it cannot tolerate North Korea's doing the same. Finally, if the United States and Korea continue to exercise patience in dealing with North Korea and concentrate all their negotiation skills on inducing North Korea to join the world community, there will surely come a time when the IAEA will be able to make North Korea or its successor a bona fide member of the NPT.

More concrete suggestions are possible on financing reunification. It is high time to organize an international study group that will explore this question. This group should include participants from the World Bank, given its mission to promote economic development in less-developed parts of the world. If launching such a group on a governmental level is considered too sensitive, a nongovernmental group may be appropriate.

With regard to institutional arrangements for the general security of Northeast Asia, a two-track approach may be considered for the time being. That is, the current US-Korean bilateral arrangement should be maintained while the two countries gradually expand the bilateral alliance into an effective multilateral alliance, which would include other powers in the region. As the military alliance between the two countries is valued more in terms of its contributions to the peace and stability of the region as a whole, it is only logical for the two countries to place their bilateral alliance in the context of a multilateral arrangement. In any event, membership in such an arrangement should be open-ended—that is, if a country in the region is willing to accept and abide by the terms and conditions agreed to by the original members, it should be allowed to join. Otherwise, the very creation of such an arrangement would contribute to instability.

It can, of course, be argued that Korea has been establishing relations with individual regional powers without much help, and the United States has been playing a balancing role in the region without the benefit of a multilateral arrangement. So why should the United States and Korea work for a multilateral arrangement? The answer, of course, is that both Korea and the United States would achieve their respective goals more easily and effectively through a multilateral arrangement: Korea would go far toward offsetting the disadvantages of its small size, and the United States would be able to mitigate its disadvantages as an outsider to the region.

And to make use of the economic dynamism of the region, each country should take greater advantage of the strengths of the other. For example, the United States should definitely make greater use of Korea's strategic location as well as its strengths in other areas. Geographically, Korea sits at the hub of the most economically dynamic region of the world. Korea also has a large market, supported by a population of more than 44 million with a per capita GNP of more than $7,000, a highly skilled labor force, a large pool of scientific and technical human resources, and an infrastructure unparalleled in any other developing country in the region. For its part, Korea should make greater use of the unrivaled technological superiority that the United States still holds and also take advantage of the vast US market.

More significantly, however, the United States seems to be trying to take advantage of the economic opportunities in the Asia-Pacific region mainly through a strengthened and upgraded Asia Pacific Economic Cooperation (APEC) forum. It is difficult to fault this approach. The Clinton administration, in particular, should be commended for having recognized APEC's potential and for having taken the initiative with the first APEC summit in Seattle in November 1993.[6]

A better approach, however, might be to combine the effort to strengthen and upgrade APEC with development of a much closer relationship with Korea. If the United States, with the consent of Canada and Mexico, offered membership in the North American Free Trade Agreement (NAFTA) to Korea and Korea accepted, the entire APEC region would rapidly turn into a genuine free trade area. Once Korea joined NAFTA, several other East Asian countries, such as Taiwan and Singapore, would also quickly join, partly because their exports are in competition with each other in the North American market. This, in turn, would encourage other countries such as Japan, Australia, New Zealand, and even ASEAN countries to seek membership. The upshot would be that the entire APEC region would become a large free trade area that would more than rival the European Union in terms of output, trade, and population. A regionwide free trade area could use its bargaining power to prod the European Union to work harder for free trade throughout the world.[7]

None of the cooperative schemes suggested above will be realized unless the two countries develop a satisfactory economic relationship. For this reason, it is appropriate to briefly assess the prospects of trade relations between the two countries over next several years and then suggest a few ways in which the two countries can improve their relations.

From the point of view of the United States, imports from Korea were the most troublesome aspect of the bilateral trade relationship in the 1980s. Sudden increases in imports of Korean industrial products not only presented

---

6. Of course, recognition of this effort should not be construed as belittling the efforts of previous US administrations to promote Asia-Pacific cooperation.

7. For a discussion of the merits of a bipolar world compared to a tripolar world, see Kim (1994, 6–7), Lee (1991), and Krause (1990, 20–25).

structural adjustment problems to the United States but also seemingly aggravated problems of balance of payments deficits. To deal with these problems, the US government employed the full range of tools available in its arsenal: antidumping charges, countervailing duties, voluntary export restraints, section 301 actions, pressure on Korea to appreciate the won, and so on.

An interesting question is whether the same kinds of problems will plague US-Korean bilateral relations in the decade ahead. Although no one can answer this question with certainty, it may be conjectured that the chances of US-Korean trade friction in this decade rising to the level of the 1980s are small at best. Much of the trade friction in the last decade basically stemmed from a mismatch of macroeconomic policies. In the early 1980s, the Reagan administration pursued policies that were termed Reaganomic in inspiration but were Keynesian in actual substance, while Korea followed policies that were Reaganomic in substance. This mismatch of policies created a kind of wind tunnel, so to speak, that sucked Korean goods into the United States (Kim 1991, 4). Now that the Cold War is over and the United States is no longer under pressure to build up its armaments, the chances of the United States pursuing simultaneous tax reductions and defense spending increases are slim. If anything, Korea is more likely to pursue a macroeconomic policy consisting of tax reductions coupled with increased social spending under the pressure of democratization.

It should also be recalled that the surge of imports from Korea was partly the result of Korea's heavy and chemical industry drive in the 1970s. Spurred by generous tax treatment and cheap credit, the drive resulted in extensive excess capacity in such industrial areas as steel, shipbuilding, machinery, automobiles, and electronics (Kim 1991, 4–5). This excess capacity, combined with policies that restricted domestic demands, forced Korean industries to increase exports to the United States, which from a US viewpoint was nothing more than dumping of exports supported by unfair government subsidies. Repetition of such a situation, however, is most unlikely as Korea rejects industrial policy practices that are inconsistent with the General Agreement on Tariffs and Trade (GATT) or the World Trade Organization (WTO) and instead emphasizes competition and deregulation.[8]

There is yet another reason why the 1990s will see less trade friction between the United States and Korea. Unlike the 1980s, Korea's export dependence on the US market is now far less than it was during the 1980s. In the mid-1980s, nearly 40 percent of Korean exports went to the United States. Now the corresponding figure is a little over 22 percent. Consequently, import surges are not likely to be a major bone of contention with the United States.

---

8. For a description of policies on deregulation by Kim Young Sam's government, see Republic of Korea (1993, esp. 87–147).

The prospect of a decline in trade friction between the United States and Korea in the 1990s will not necessarily mean that there will be no friction whatsoever. As the two economies become more interlinked through globalization, many frictions will arise due to what one might call systemic differences. To address these problems, the two countries should, of course, make increasing use of the Dialogue for Economic Cooperation (DEC) framework agreed to at the Kim-Clinton summit in Seoul in July 1993.

But this suggestion does not go very far, for two reasons. Unless renewed, the DEC was to have expired in June 1994.[9] What is more important, the DEC has been too concerned with problems that have already arisen—that is, putting out fires rather than preventing them. To identify and eliminate systemic or structural impediments to trade in advance, the two countries may agree to launch what will amount to an improved version of the Structural Impediments Initiative (SII) talks that were conducted between the United States and Japan several years ago. However, the US-Japan model requires at least two improvements: it should have a more positive name—perhaps the Initiative for Structural Harmonization, or ISH,[10] and the business communities should have greater input.[11] The basic purpose of the talks should not be to negotiate each step of market opening through hard bargaining, but rather to provide mutual assistance toward making the respective economic systems more compatible. Needless to say, such talks would also go a long way toward preparing Korea for membership in NAFTA.

Summary and Conclusion

The end of the Cold War has brought about significant changes in the domestic and external policies of the United States and Korea. Despite these changes, the two countries need each other now more than ever.

The United States and Korea should address key issues in their bilateral relations concerning moves to end the Cold War on the Korean peninsula, Korea's establishment of good relations with its large neighbors, and the need for the United States to play the role of balancer in the region. In addition, both countries need to increase their competitiveness in order to make better use of the economic dynamism of the Asia-Pacific region. In

---

9. The Korean and US governments did in fact agree to terminate the DEC. However, they agreed to file a joint report on the accomplishments of the DEC and use the following 12 months to implement what the two countries had agreed upon to further reduce barriers to trade and investment.

10. C. Fred Bergsten suggested this during the discussion that followed the author's presentation of this paper.

11. Lawrence Krause suggested that the talks should be carried out between the business communities of the two countries rather than the governments.

addressing all these challenges, there is a high degree of compatibility in the two countries' interests.

The most immediate task in meeting those challenges is to deal with the development of North Korea's nuclear capabilities, and the United States and Korea must continue to exercise the utmost patience. Apart from this task, the two countries might launch a study group to explore ways of financing reunification. They also should harmonize the structure of their economies while thinking about placing the current bilateral security arrangement in the multilateral regional context. The United States, together with Canada and Mexico, should consider offering Korea membership in NAFTA. Korean membership will surely start a process whereby other East Asian countries such as Taiwan and Singapore will join, making the whole APEC region a de facto free trade area. As such, an enlarged NAFTA could easily rival the European Union in influence. An enlarged NAFTA and the European Union together could, in turn, work for global free trade. In short, in this global age, a US-Korean partnership, imaginatively developed, has immense potential not only for enhancing the well-being of their own peoples but also that of people throughout the world.

References

Eberstadt, Nicholas. 1992. "Can the Two Koreas Be One?" *Foreign Affairs* 72, no. 5.

Kim, Kihwan. 1990. "Deregulating the Domestic Economy: Korea's Experience in the 1980s." Presented at the Senior Policy Seminar, sponsored by the Economic Development Institute and the World Bank, Caracas, Venezuela, 19–22 July.

Kim, Kihwan. 1991. "The Political Economy of U.S.-Korea Trade Friction in the 1980s: A Korean Perspective." Presented at the Hoover Conference on US-Korea Economic Relations, Stanford, California, 5–7 December.

Kim, Kihwan. 1994. "Pacific Economic Cooperation: Outlook and Agenda for the 1990s." In *The Pacific Century: Scenarios for Regional Cooperation*. Westport, CT: Greenwood Publishing Group, Inc.

Krause, Lawrence B., and Mark Sundberg. 1990. "Inter-Relationship Between the World and Pacific Economic Performance." Photocopy of revised paper (February).

Lee, Kuan Yew. 1991. "Asia Pacific: A Bullish Scenario Relies on Partnership." *International Herald Tribune* (24 June).

Lee, Young Sun. 1992. "Economic Integration in the Korean Peninsula: A Scenario Approach to the Cost of Unification." Prepared for the Second Washington Conference on Korea-America Economic Association, sponsored by the American Enterprise Institute for Public Policy Research, Washington, 28–29 September.

Noland, Marcus. 1993. "U.S. Trade Policy Toward Asia." Prepared for the conference on Economic Cooperation in the Asia-Pacific Community, Seoul, 10–12 November.

Republic of Korea Government. 1993. *New Five-Year Economic Plan 1993–1997*. Seoul.

US International Trade Commission. 1993. *East Asia: Regional Economic Integration and Implications for the United States*. USITC Publication 2621. Washington (May).

Whalley, John. 1992. "The Uruguay Round and the GATT: Whither the Global System?" Prepared for the PAFTAD 20 conference, Pacific Dynamism and the International Economic System, Washington, 10–12 September.

4

An American Perspective

LAWRENCE B. KRAUSE

Two major forces are driving the world economy: the end of the Cold War and technological advances. I will discuss both. The overall context in which US-Korean economic relations must be analyzed has drastically changed. Indeed, the analysis of any international economic relationship must begin with the consequences of the end of the Cold War because it constitutes a watershed for the world economy. Every country and every firm has been affected by it.

The political economy of relations between the United States and Korea fully reflects the change. Several implications are well-recognized and will require little argumentation. Four will be noted: the elevation of economic relations, the promotion of regional at the expense of multilateral economic relations, the differential effect among countries, and the pressure for business restructuring.

First, the end of the Cold War has elevated economic relative to traditional security concerns in international relations. This is reflected in official US government agenda setting. In his 1994 State of the Union message, President Clinton spent less than 5 out of 66 minutes discussing security concerns, including the nuclear issue with North Korea. Rather, domestic economic and social issues dominate the agenda. And since the administration has linked domestic economic health so closely to international markets, it follows that international economic relations have risen in importance.

Lawrence B. Krause is Pacific Economic Cooperation Professor and director of the Korea-Pacific Program, Graduate School of International Relations and Pacific Studies, University of California, San Diego.

Second, the Cold War's end has promoted regional at the expense of multilateral economic relations. When representatives of the world economy as a whole are assembled, as they were during the recently concluded negotiations of the General Agreement on Tariffs and Trade, the diversity of countries and their interests are apparent. Unless there is a hegemon to force compromises at its own expense (that is, to pay for the public good) as the United States did in the past, then only minimal agreements can be reached, such as the disappointing Uruguay Round. In my view, this will be the last time such a negotiation will be attempted. At the same time, however, cross-border economic activity is becoming even more critical for economic growth of countries and individual firms. The resolution of this apparent conflict of forces is regionalism—a pulling together of countries with similar economic interests. In my view, there will be only two megaregions: the European Union and the Asia Pacific Economic Cooperation (APEC) countries. This is very important to US-Korean relations, as both countries are in the APEC region.

What about the impact of the North American Free Trade Agreement on US-Korean economic relations? Unlike the European Union, APEC permits subgroups such as the ASEAN Free Trade Area (AFTA) and NAFTA, and therefore the United States can promote NAFTA and APEC simultaneously. The passage of NAFTA by the US Congress gave a strong message to Korea that the United States will continue its outward-oriented economic strategy rather than retreating into a protectionist shell. At the same time, it cements the special relationship, due to geography and history, between Mexico and the United States. The enlargement of the US market is more of an opportunity than a challenge for Korean firms. The opening of the Mexican market and the option of locating direct investments there is much more valuable to Korea than is the increased competition that will be coming from Mexican producers. US policy seems to be on a tack of negotiating trade agreements with countries with which it has a special relationship. Because Korea is special to the United States, some sort of trade agreement should be contemplated, though the NAFTA model is probably not the correct route.

Third, the end of the Cold War has meant different things to different countries; there have been winners and losers. Obviously, the biggest loser by far has been the Soviet Union/Russia. Another loser in the short to medium term has been Germany because it bungled the reunification of East Germany so badly. Germany's loss is critical because it has spilled over to the rest of Europe. Another modest loser has been Japan, which has lost its free-ride status not only in narrow military terms, but also with respect to its ability to shirk international economic and political responsibilities.

Gainers include the Republic of Korea and the United States. Korea gained because its difficult transition to a civilian presidency was not encumbered by external forces, and it gained mightily relative to North

Korea. Korea has the distinct advantage of being able to apply lessons from the German experience to its own inevitable reunification. The United States has been a moderate winner because it has been relieved of the crushing burden of military expenditure that competition with the Soviet Union made necessary. Of course, the shift to a civilian production structure has necessitated painful and difficult adjustments (not unlike those of 1945–46), but on balance the opportunities outweigh the challenges.

However, the largest gainer has been China. China has been relieved of the security threat along its long land border, its political system no longer is a barrier to full economic interchange and integration with the rest of the world, and the universal rejection of central planning has made further market-oriented reforms acceptable within China. The rise of China relative to Japan is having profound effects throughout the Pacific Basin. APEC now has three large powers as members: China, Japan, and the United States, and this has increased the importance of both Korea and ASEAN as balancers. Strategic business decisions in the United States and Korea must take into account both China and Japan; neither can be ignored.

The increasing economic importance of China can hardly be over-emphasized. China is the fastest-growing country in the world. It is already the third largest in terms of aggregate GDP, and it could displace Japan in the second spot if current trends continue. The full entry of China into world markets is a daunting prospect for firms everywhere. Chinese workers can be energetic, educable, and cheap—and there are so many of them. More than half of all Chinese workers are still small-scale farmers. It will be some time before all surplus labor is enticed from agriculture into industry, so a decided upward trend in Chinese industrial wages is far off in the future. Thus, China will be very competitive in labor-intensive processes for some time.

Multinational firms can unravel the production of almost all goods and isolate a labor-intensive portion—usually assembly operations. For those products whose production runs are long, firms will increasingly locate the labor-intensive portions in China. India and possibly Vietnam could be in similar positions. Thus, firms will need to have a presence in China not only to produce standard products for world markets, but also to sell to the increasingly lucrative Chinese market. Firms will need to adopt a niche strategy for production elsewhere with multipurpose production facilities and systems. They will concentrate on newer products and processes. Of course, this is an exaggerated picture: not all standard products will be made in China. Some of China's competitive edge will be lost to transportation costs and lengthy response times. However, the central point remains. Advanced countries will increasingly become producers of service-oriented goods.

Another factor related to the end of the Cold War needs to be mentioned—namely, that it is also a watershed for North Korea (the Democratic People's Republic of Korea, or DPRK)—one with serious negative consequences. North Korea lost its principal ally with the Soviet Union's dissolution, which ended both economic and military assistance. China has also ended its economic preferences for North Korea and limits military cooperation. The Warsaw Pact has dissolved, and these countries also ended economic relations with North Korea.

Thus, North Korea has been forced to rely on domestic production, which is ironic since it always glorified self-sufficiency (*juche*) but is ill-suited for it, being too small and lacking petroleum resources. Estimates indicate that its per capita income has been falling rapidly and may have reached the levels of the early 1970s. North Korea must recognize that time is against it: every year, the economic gap between it and South Korea widens, and the military is following a similar trajectory. This is a very unsettling atmosphere in which to go through the change in leadership following the death of Kim Il Sung.

The fourth factor arising from the Cold War's end is the pressure on business firms worldwide to restructure. Firms are going through a revolutionary change—whether it be called restructuring, reengineering, or simply rethinking, it is universal. The revolution can be linked to the end of the Cold War because it began with firms that depended on government military contracts, both hardware and software enterprises. Once their managers realized that new contracts were going to be few and far between, they began to shed superfluous plant and employees. They were forced to compete for civilian business, and they realized they had to become "lean and mean." The firms in neighboring industries immediately recognized that they faced increased competition and began their own belt tightening. From that point, capital markets took over and demanded that firms restructure. Those that announced job elimination and selling of peripheral businesses were rewarded with higher equity evaluations. Those that resisted the trend—possibly because the firms were doing fairly well—found that their shares were underperforming the market. Since managers take the maximizing of shareholder value seriously, they could not resist the trend. Hence, it has not been unusual for firms to report record profits and plans to eliminate jobs simultaneously. American firms are well-advanced in this process and Korean firms less so.

Technology-Driven Economic Development

The other factor that characterizes the world economy is that technological advances are the dominant influence determining economic growth in all countries except those in the earliest stages of industrial catchup. As is discussed below, this factor constitutes the basic rationale for an industrial alliance between Korea and the United States.

While it is hard to establish empirically, certainly the perception exists that the pace of technological change is speeding up. Furthermore, technological advances are breaking down preexisting distinctions between industries such as electronics and telecommunications. The pace and character of technological change is reinforcing the wisdom of outward-oriented, market-conforming policies because no country can isolate itself from these developments and prosper. At the same time, technological advances are becoming harder to achieve, forcing policymakers to rethink their approach and in some cases to create explicit policy where none had existed.

These technological trends have turned old antitrust laws into anachronisms. Rapid technological change makes the existence of a purely competitive market impossible. Major shares of a domestic market may be necessary for survival. Pricing at marginal cost is a formula for bankruptcy, as development costs are not recovered. Pricing is a strategic decision of firms; they are clearly not price takers. While there may well be anticompetitive actions by firms that public policy should proscribe, they are not related to size, which was the touchstone in the past. More likely, such anticompetitive actions are related to discriminatory pricing, which makes the antidumping laws the most important policy instrument. Since antidumping laws can be abused for protective purposes, they have become a significant policy area for international negotiations.

Oligopoly is the rule rather than the exception. While there are differences among industries, oligopolies tend to be unstable, as the position of individual firms can reverse with a technological breakthrough and a new entrant can be created through cross-industry mergers. Hence, competition between participants in the oligopoly can be keen.

While the terminology is somewhat misleading, I believe the term "managed trade" is the best way to characterize the international trade regime that technological change dictates. Trade is managed primarily by individual firms, usually involving foreign direct investment. Much of what is reported as international trade is between a parent and a subsidiary abroad. Groups of firms and trade associations are also part of the management of trade flows. Governments are also involved to a lesser degree, and more through indirect policies rather than border restrictions. What is clear is that international trade has become even more important for economic advance. No country has the human and financial resources to be at the forefront of all technologies all of the time. The bottom line is that growth will be determined by market size and technological advance, which will rest on the amount and quality of education provided to the population.

What technologies have been the most dynamic recently? Fifteen years ago, the US National Academy of Sciences identified five technologies that would be critical in the coming decades: biotechnology, material sciences, microelectronics, robotics, and telecommunications. This has turned out to be a remarkably accurate forecast. The academy did underestimate the importance of software advances, which have made giant strides. These technologies are important not only in and of themselves but because they touch almost all sectors of the economy.

The reaction of businesses to these technological changes has been varied, but all successful firms have reacted strongly. Some have restructured by specializing or downsizing. Most have improved their skills in scanning the technological capabilities of direct competitors and in neighboring industries that may intrude upon their domain. Increasingly, they have formed industrial alliances to improve their competitive position.

Industrial Alliances

An industrial alliance is something more than just a distribution agreement, a cross-licensing of technology agreement, or a joint venture for marketing, production, or R&D, although it may involve all these things. It is an agreement to create an ongoing business relationship based on trust and mutual benefit that forms a framework for cooperation in order to improve the competitive position of both parties while maintaining the separate managerial and ownership identity of both. Industrial alliances represent a long-term viewpoint and a willingness to invest in a relationship (Lorange and Roos 1992). The agreement may be more of an understanding rather than a contract, and it is created step by step with successive joint endeavors. This means it can be interrupted or ended by either party. Successful industrial alliances lead to a high degree of interdependence between the participants. Firms are wise enough to know that every venture will not be successful and that there are always unexpected occurrences. However, they do not expect, nor will they tolerate, being taken advantage of, nor countenance government interference that tilts the balance against them. Since trust is at the center of the alliance, personal relationships are heavily involved. This may well mean close working relationships between technicians as well as managers.

Three forces motivate the creation of industrial alliances. First, the increasing cost, complexity, and risk of developing new technologies are forcing firms to find ways to share risk. Second, firms must compete in global markets, and they need help in cracking them. Third, many new and powerful foreign competitors are being created. Firms are seeking help in remaining at the top of their industries. As noted in the preface to *Technology Transfer in Consortia and Strategic Alliances* (Gibson and Smilor 1992), technology companies are forming strategic alliances to meet increasing international competition, to cope with the rising cost of advanced research, to leverage scarce scientific and technical talent, and to share risks associated with technology generation and commercialization.

Because firms must operate in principle in all important regions of the world and sometimes in several industries, they will not form an exclusive industrial alliance with any one firm and may form several. Firms will likely seek industrial alliances with major competitors in foreign countries. For US firms, that may mean industrial alliances with Japanese and German firms, as well as with others. For Korean firms, alliances with American, Japanese, and German firms may all be attractive.

US-Korean Relations in an Era of Industrial Alliances

The United States and South Korea have maintained a mutually beneficial political and security alliance for over 40 years, but as already noted, the world has changed. However, these new circumstances (as well as an old one) only reinforce the need for a close relationship between the Republic of Korea and the United States. The old circumstance is the continuing security threat posed by North Korea. Since this has been the basis for the successful US-Korean military alliance for 40 years and both governments recognize and have reiterated support for it, there is no reason to believe that the military alliance will change until the threat is removed (Lee 1993).

Korea and the United States need each other. For Korea, the geopolitical and historical context of the country suggests that the United States is the best friend that Korea can have among the major powers. This is the argument put forth by Jin-Hyun Kim (1993). For the United States, the growing economic power of China along with that of Japan and the prospects of Russia in the wings suggests a complex exercise of power in East Asia in which a strong Korea is needed for regional balance. Korea is the country that promises the most enduring relationship with the United States and one whose interests are likely to be most compatible with those of the United States.

We can think of industrial alliances as extending cooperation already forged in security matters into the domain of industry. The Asia-Pacific region promises to be the most dynamic and competitive in the world. Hence, firms in both the United States and Korea have reason to seek cooperation and alliances. However, much needs to be done before the concept of a relationship strengthened by industrial alliances can become a reality.

Rationale for an Industrial Alliance

Alliances among governments are usually formed for a specific purpose, such as improving the competence and thus the competitiveness of companies in a particular product line, service, or process. A critical ingredient in all alliances is the necessity for mutual benefits or gains. Sang-Mok Suh has described the mutual gains from an industrial alliance as "filling the gaps in the industrial structure for each other."

Identifying gaps that firms in the partner country might fill cannot be done in the abstract; industrial cooperation requires analysis of particular industries, or even firms. The gaps that Korean firms or industries most likely face and that American partners can fill involve technology. A second motivation on the Korean side is gaining access to the worldwide marketing channels of US multinational corporations (Jung 1992).

The corresponding gap on the American side that Korean firms could fill may be of several kinds. Probably the most important is the manufacturing skills of Korean firms, particularly in mass production of standard products. They have made significant gains in engineering and quality control. Thus, Korea may provide a lower-cost production base to serve Asian markets such as Japan. Korea has a locational advantage in reaching north China and parts of Russia as well as Japan. Korean firms can also be invaluable in helping American firms penetrate the Korean market and can provide financial capital. Moreover, as Korean firms increase their competence in R&D, they can be a valuable partner in technology exchange.

Getting from Here to There

Many American firms have already formed partnerships with Korean firms, and a significant number have been unsatisfactory for the American side. The problem must be addressed if future industrial alliances are to be formed. This is not to suggest that there are no success stories. The joint ventures between Posco and USX and between Caltex and Lucky-Goldstar quickly come to mind. There are also legitimate complaints on the Korean side. Nevertheless, Dow Chemical, Gulf Oil, and General Motors have made highly visible disinvestments that will not soon be forgotten, and the issues that they raise cannot be ignored. The problems and complaints have been documented and publicized (American Chamber of Commerce in Korea 1993): inadequate protection of intellectual property rights, inadequate and restricted access to the Korean market, and excessive government interference with business that works disproportionately against foreign firms. Other complaints could be added but are rather well-known.

In my view, the basic root of the problem is that Korea has not come to grips with how to relate to foreigners in the face of a global economy and global competition. Korea displays a strong distrust of all foreigners (some more than others). While understandable given Korea's history, this attitude is an insurmountable barrier. Korean government bureaucrats do not want foreign firms to succeed in Korea. They appear to believe that the government tolerates relations with foreign firms for the sole purpose of gaining access to technology; once the technology is mastered, the foreigner should be tossed out. One hears statements that Korea should not be dependent on foreign firms for its critical technology.

But technological independence is impossible for any country. Even the United States and Japan lack sufficient human and financial resources to lead in all necessary industrial technologies all of the time. Striving for complete technological independence will only make the situation worse for Korea, since foreign firms will be very reluctant to transfer technology to Korea under these terms. If they do agree to the transfer, the foreign firms must then price their technology in Korea as if they were selling it for fear that the technology will be appropriated and taken out of their control. And as firms will not sell their critical technologies, these are simply not being made available to Korean firms.

Of course, Korean firms are making some strides in indigenous technology development; such successes are essential to its international competitiveness. With that technology, Korean firms can make cross-licensing agreements to gain access to yet more advanced technology. It can thus make technical progress but not become technologically independent. Indeed, Korean firms will become interdependent with foreign firms and will transfer technology abroad, as well as receiving it. Yet Korea as yet does not appear comfortable with this vision.

There are also some distinct shortcomings on the American side. Too many American firms have too much faith in the superiority of the technology that they have developed and the manufacturing skills they have achieved. This creates a closed mind-set that hinders learning and forecloses opportunities for inward technology transfer. Furthermore, American firms may not appreciate the implication of cultural differences and are unwilling to adapt to other cultures. In truth, Asian business practices, which place more importance on personal relationships, are better preparation for the industrial alliances that will dominate the next decade. Hence, American firms must learn from Korean firms as well as the reverse. Just as in government-to-government relations, American and Korean firms must learn how to establish equitable relations.

Role of Government in Industrial Alliances

Beginning most actively in 1961, the Korean government has been a participant in designing and running the economy. While some moderation has occurred in the early 1980s, Korea is still much more intrusive than most other governments. It is widely recognized in Korea that this must change, and the Kim Young Sam government initiated much reform in 1993. Much is still needed, however, especially in the area of finance. Korea is further behind in financial technology than it was 20 years ago. Both domestic firms and foreign firms wanting to operate in Korea suffer because of the backwardness of its financial markets and institutions, and this is a major limitation to Korea's international competitiveness.

On the other hand, the US government must intrude more in the running of its economy. It cannot rely on markets alone. The government ought to be more involved in organizing cooperative research efforts and improving the basic infrastructure of the economy, especially in education.

If the Korean government does what it must do—that is, liberalize—and the US government does what it must do—that is, take more direct responsibility for the competitiveness of industry—then the two governments will be on a path of convergence. This will improve understanding between the two and improve their relationship.

The Korean government has begun to implement the idea of an industrial alliance between Korea and the United States, as proposed by Minister Kim Chul-Su when he visited Washington, DC, in April 1993. In addition to rhetorical support, a fund has been established to help small and medium-sized Korean firms get involved in alliances.

The US government has reacted coolly to the proposal, both because officials are unsure what it means and also because they believe that the business environment in Korea needs to be improved before US firms will consider alliances. Nevertheless, the US government does have policy instruments addressed to small and medium-sized firms that could be harnessed to alliances if that was seen as desirable. The current US position should not be considered a rejection, but rather a neutral reaction. The most critical action both governments can take to promote alliances is to improve the atmosphere for doing international business.

Other things must also be done to manage the relationship better. Disputes are inevitable in any close relationship. The US side will continue to complain of limitations to market access, and the Korean side will complain about antidumping actions with protectionist intent. Therefore, a better dispute settlement mechanism should be explored, either within or outside the APEC framework. The principles to guide the relationship are straightforward. An equal relationship is marked by reciprocity and national treatment.

Conclusions

Korea is in the process of joining the ranks of advanced nations. Symbolically, this graduation is marked by its prospective entry into the Organization for Economic Cooperation and Development. This change in Korea heralds an end to disputes such as that raised over Korean production and export of photo albums because those kinds of industries will no longer exist in Korea. It will also mean that agriculture will be seen as a socio-political issue and not an economic one, making the issue more manageable.

On the other hand, Korea will be entering a new era in which reciprocity and national treatment will be expected. Korean financial markets will have to be opened to foreign firms. Korea cannot expect to be an exporter of automobiles without opening its domestic market to competition from foreign suppliers. Such changes are not made without difficulty, but Korea's new status will require them.

The most dramatic change, however, will come in the firm-to-firm relationships that Korean businesses will establish with foreign companies. These relationships are likely to be marked by many industrial alliances. Korea will be able to choose among many possible affiliations. I believe US firms hold the most promise, but that must be proved.

It is also true, however, that US firms have many alternative choices for partners in industrial alliances. The atmosphere for doing business in Korea must improve if Korea is to be a desirable choice. The governments can promote or retard this development, so government policy must be scrutinized to make sure it is supportive.

Finally, the bilateral economic relationship between Korea and the United States will be embedded in a regional context. Increasingly, APEC will be important for both countries. If the bilateral relationship is sound and properly managed, then the regional context can only solidify the link.

References

American Chamber of Commerce in Korea. 1993. *US-Korea Trade Issues* (March).

Gibson, David, and Raymond W. Smilor, editors. 1992. *Technology Transfer in Consortia and Strategic Alliances*. Lanham, MD: Rowman & Littlefield.

Jung, Ku-Hyun. 1992. "Strategic Business Alliance Between Korea and the US." A Report of the Model Joint Venture Study Submitted to the Korea US Business Council (June).

Kim, Jin-Hyun. 1993. "Korea and the World: Asia-Pacific Dynamism." Michigan State University, 7–11 July.

Lee, Chae-Jin. 1993. "US Policy Toward South Korea." In Donald N. Clark, *Korea Briefing*. New York and Boulder, CO: Asia Society, Westview Press.

Lorange, Peter, and Johan Roos. 1992. *Strategic Alliances*. Cambridge, MA: Blackwell (Business).

III

THE UNITED STATES AND KOREA
IN THE ASIA-PACIFIC REGION

5

A Korean Perspective

SOOGIL YOUNG

Even by the early 1980s, Asia was hardly a region, except in the geographic sense. Politically and economically, Asia was more like an archipelago, with each heavily dependent on the United States for security, capital, technology, and markets, among other things. As a result, there existed a hub-and-spoke pattern of interdependence in the Asia-Pacific region, with the United States as the hub and the Asian countries as spokes.

The spokes in this pattern of trans-Pacific interdependence included Korea, Taiwan, Hong Kong, and Singapore, which emerged in the 1980s as probably the world's most dynamic economies. These so-called newly industrialized economies (NIEs) of Asia achieved their success by following export-led growth strategies, taking advantage of their partnerships with the United States in doing so.

Korea's experiences highlight the common key elements in the success of these economies. Korea's export-led growth strategy consisted of the promotion of exports, encouragement of inflow of foreign capital and technology, and promotion of infant industries. These were not enough, however. The strategy would not have worked but for the following three additional components: a good human capital base, the open global trading system, and, probably most important, continued domestic reform efforts.

Such reforms—including the strengthening of market mechanisms and the opening of domestic markets—were necessary on a continuing basis to

Soogil Young, an international economist, is currently president of the Korea Transport Institute in Seoul.

maintain export-led economic growth and the inflow of foreign capital. Liberalization of markets and trade policy has always been one of the principal tenets of Korea's economic policies. For sure, the country started out with a very high level of government intervention in the markets as well as high import barriers to protect its infant industries, but both have been continually reduced.

Further, the export-led growth strategy would not have worked if the industrial partner countries, principally the United States, had not underwritten those efforts. The United States granted Korea most-favored nation access to its vast domestic markets, and it also provided access to capital and technologies. These policies, extended not only to Korea but also to other developing countries in and outside the Asia-Pacific region, were part of the United States' Cold War strategy to hedge against the communist bloc.

The economic success of Korea, Taiwan, Hong Kong, and Singapore was the first phase of a broader East Asian phenomenon. Emulating the experiences of these economies, Malaysia, Thailand, Indonesia, and China also began to pursue the outward-oriented development strategy and soon emerged as the second tier of the Asian NIEs. East Asia including Japan has thus been the most dynamic region in the world.

The region's economic growth in East Asia accelerated during the second half of the 1980s due in large measure to rising flows of investment into and among the East Asian economies. These investment flows in turn increased the trading activities of these economies, particularly intraregional trade flows. As a result, even in the absence of an institutional scheme for regional integration, East Asia has become a closely interdependent economic region in this sense. The market mechanism triggered by each nation's voluntary reforms to attract foreign capital was the underlying impetus behind this regional integration. Consequently, the hub-and-spoke pattern of trans-Pacific interdependence has been replaced by a mosaic of Asia-Pacific interdependence, with intraregional trade exceeding extraregional trade in volume.

This means, among other things, that the East Asian economies' dependence on the United States as an export market is no longer as high as it has been. Whereas the United States once exceeded East Asia by far in terms of the share of regional exports it received while Japan and the developing economies of East Asia accounted for 16 percent and 10 percent, respectively, in 1992, the United States accounted for only 24 percent while Japan and developing East Asia accounted for 15 percent and 25 percent, respectively. In addition, developing East Asia has become a larger market for Korea than is the United States.

The ascendancy of developing East Asia as a new and dynamic growth pole of the world economy has been accompanied by the emergence of serious and recurrent trade disputes between the East Asian developing economies and the United States, which no longer tolerates developing

East Asian economies' barriers to trade. The United States has threatened retaliation to press these economies to open their domestic markets to US goods and services. These countries usually have acceded to US demands, but only reluctantly and after protracted, acrimonious negotiations.

The US trade offensive—so-called aggressive unilateralism—has had considerable effect in encouraging these East Asian economies to liberalize trade. At the same time, however, this policy has had its costs—namely, in terms of US loss of East Asians' goodwill and its political capital in the region. The United States lost many East Asians' trust because its aggressive unilateralism was seen as a willful and therefore unfair imposition of arbitrarily defined norms. No doubt, one of the motivating factors behind the Malaysian proposal of an East Asian Economic Group, which subsequently became an East Asian Economic Caucus (EAEC), was this resentment.

The successful conclusion of the Uruguay Round notwithstanding, trans-Pacific trade tensions are likely to resume and persist, for at least two reasons. First, at the bottom of trans-Pacific trade tensions are the adjustment difficulties that the dynamically expanding economies of East Asia continue to impose on the United States. This will continue as long as the East Asian economies' dynamic expansion continues. Second, liberalization of the East Asian economies, though steady, will remain gradual and too slow to satisfy the United States.

In coping with protectionism in East Asia, the United States will be tempted to continue using aggressive unilateralism. This approach may backfire, however, sparking an anti-American move at a forum such as the EAEC. At the same time, aggressive unilateralism is unlikely to be effective. As already noted, the United States' influence will continue to decline as it becomes a relatively less important trade partner and as East Asian trade partners increase in importance to each other. Consequently, US threats of unilateral trade sanctions will carry less weight. In addition, increasingly globalized East Asian economies can more easily bypass US retaliatory import barriers, which are likely to hurt the domestic producers as much as foreign exporters.

Trade liberalization is not the only way to promote trade, however. It may not even be the best way. Trade may be facilitated through investment and its liberalization, harmonization of standards and competition policies, macroeconomic policies, resolution of disputes, better circulation of information, as well as better marketing. There is ample room in these areas for bilateral cooperation or in the context of regional cooperation in the Asia-Pacific region. The best forum for these efforts is Asia Pacific Economic Cooperation (APEC). Work in these areas may in fact be the most important work APEC can do.

Trade liberalization is still important, of course. But it should ideally be promoted at the global level. Korea and the United States should continue to work together toward global trade negotiations through the World Trade Organization, which will come into being with the beginning of 1995.

The formation of a free trade area (FTA) in the Asia-Pacific region can complement the global effort for trade liberalization provided such an agreement is open to any country willing to assume membership obligations. However, an Asia-Pacific free trade area may not be feasible if some regional countries fail to join. China is not a market economy, and this is likely to impede its ability to join. Even if this were not so, China might refuse to join because it is politically impossible to do so. The same is true of the members of the Association of Southeast Asian Nations (ASEAN). The ASEAN Free Trade Area (AFTA) illustrates the difficulty that many developing countries would have in joining an FTA. AFTA covers only manufactured goods, and for many of these goods, even in 15 years tariffs will not drop below 5 percent. Should either China or Southeast Asian countries or both fail to join an Asia-Pacific free trade area while other regional countries join, trade will be diverted away from the excluded developing economies, squandering the dynamism of these economies to the detriment of all regional economies.

If China and Southeast Asian countries refuse to join in the proposed free trade area, Japan may also refuse. Alternatively, the United States may block Japan's admittance out of a belief that Japanese trade barriers are not amenable to negotiated removal. In this case, Japan may exercise its influence on those developing economies so that they may not join either. If this were to happen, Japan and other nonparticipating countries might collude to set up discriminatory trade barriers against the members of the free trade area, in effect creating two trading blocs in the Asia-Pacific region and thereby undermining the economic dynamism of the region as a whole.

Other options for regional economic integration include bilateral accession to the North American Free Trade Agreement and formation of EAEC. In the case of NAFTA, Korea should not join unless two conditions are met. First, there should be a reasonable assurance that its joining will lead, in the not-too-distant future, to the enlargement of NAFTA into a regionwide free trade area, including China and the Southeast Asian countries. Second, a hub-and-spoke system of Asia-Pacific free trade agreements should be avoided. Such a system benefits the hub country but hurts the spoke countries in their economic relations with each other.

Formation of the EAEC may not be desirable because it would undermine APEC and thus become a divisive voice in the Asia-Pacific region. However, once EAEC becomes a reality, Korea should not hesitate to join so it can push for freer, nondiscriminatory trade in the Asia-Pacific region.

A consensus among the Asia-Pacific countries in favor of a regionwide free trade area is what is most desirable. Therefore, US-Korean cooperation for freer trade in the Asia-Pacific region must take the form of regionwide discussions rather than a bilateral negotiation. In the meantime, Korea and the United States should promote industrial cooperation by encouraging mutual and joint investment in order to enhance each other's international competitiveness.

6

An American Perspective

RUDIGER DORNBUSCH

Four developments make it particularly timely to assess US interests and goals in the Asia-Pacific region and the role Korean-US relations play in that context:

■ The Cold War has ended, and a power vacuum has arisen from the breakup of the Soviet Union, along with the subsequent meltdown of Russia and the uncertain posture of a post-hyperinflation Russia.

■ China has emerged as an economic superperformer and as a super-power by virtue of its sheer size. The United States needs to go beyond its focus nuclear nonproliferation, human rights, protectionism, and haggling over most-favored nation (MFN) status and develop a positive approach that gives China room in the world economy while keeping up strong pressures for political opening.

■ A new taste for regionalism has been fostered, not only by European integration in the common market and its pending extension to the East and by the conclusion of the North American Free Trade Agreement (NAFTA), but also by the limitations to GATT processes in reaping further deep, fast, and broad trade opening.

■ A frustrating stalemate, which brings more disappointments as Japan's bureaucracy and politicians refuse to live up to international responsibilities and commitments, continues in US-Japanese relations. There is a

Rudiger Dornbusch is Ford International Professor of Economics at the Massachusetts Institute of Technology.

possibility that Japan will emerge from its internal political troubles and these external confrontations as an unfriendly country. Just as France fears where Germany will move, Korea and other Asian economies must be wary of a Japan that has lost its stability.

The November 1993 meeting of the Asia Pacific Economic Cooperation (APEC) forum highlighted the need for and willingness of the United States to focus on US economic relations with Asia and develop a forward-looking agenda. The Bergsten blueprint for US relations with the Asian economies—whether for lack of administration preparedness or simply on its merits—set the agenda for the next few years. US-Korean relations can play a special role in that context.

Economics and Security

The disappearance of the Soviet Union as a credible, immediate threat creates a major vacuum in Asian power relations. Of course, Russia is not gone and, judging from the instability and rumblings we have witnessed there, will not be a stable Western European power. In fact, it is quite plausible that Russia will emerge as an unstable and nationalistic power that is far less predictable than in the past.

There is a second power vacuum created out of the ambiguity in US interests in Asia; the willingness to defend them is surely in question. Even where there are formal commitments, one wonders how great the enthusiasm would be to defend Japan, for instance. Finally, the emergence of China as a regional superpower is a reality even if for the time being it retains much of the character of a less developed nation.

Thus, a peace dividend in Asia is unlikely. Japan is likely to rearm, further and formally, to face perceived or real Korean and Chinese threats. Korea will be concerned with reemerging Russian threats, a rearmed Japan, and an overwhelmingly powerful China. Uncertainties loom especially large because the role of the United States as a security umbrella must be questioned. In the past, any conflict was likely to involve Russia, and that meant a global conflict from which the United States could not stand back. That is not necessarily the case for future conflicts. Accordingly, the extent to which the United States is willing to act as a policeman is in question.

The United States does not have a functioning Asia policy. Old security commitments, based on the conflicts of the past and taking US willingness to intervene for granted, are outdated. The overriding interest today is economic. Success in that area may foster common interests that ultimately can become the basis for a new regional security arrangement. Failure to build stronger ties, on the other hand, may help US security commitments to wither even more, setting the stage for a power play among nations in the region.

The Bilateral Imbalance

The United States runs a major bilateral deficit with Asia and with virtually every Asian economy (figure 1). Part of the story, without doubt, is the US budget deficit and its reflection in a general external deficit. But part is also an Asian mercantilist strategy that relies on cautious market opening and conscious preservation of undervalued currencies.

Specifically, as the appreciation of the yen relative to the dollar is sustained and pushed further, there should be no excuse for Asian economies not to move very substantially with the yen. So far, Asian appreciation has not had that pattern (table 1). Certainly, yen appreciation should not lead to another round of export-led growth and opportunity for the Asian winners. Although the United States will find little support in the region for a general Asian real appreciation—differentiated by countries and led by Japan—it should be an objective the United States fights hard for and by all available means. It is in the end a far more generalized means of opening markets than the trench warfare of the past decade.

US-Japan Problems

For more than a decade, the United States and everybody else have been frustrated with the lack of success in opening Japan's markets. The negotiations have amounted to an unending sequence of frustrations: hard-won agreements never kept, an often unjustified blaming for the lack of results on the inferior quality of US goods, the laziness of US firms, and the US twin deficits.

Whatever the merits of these arguments, by now it is clear that there is also a layer of hardcore implicit and administrative protection at work in Japan. This is obvious from the performance of world-class US firms that do exceptionally well elsewhere but can't get a foot in the door in Japan. But it would be a mistake to limit the argument to the most competitive US firms or even to the United States. The overall picture of Japan is of an extraordinarily closed economy in manufacturing trade unlike any other (table 2). It is true in manufacturing and even more so in services.

The argument that Japan is different—that it needs to export in order to finance oil imports—is, of course, absurd. Certainly it needs to export, but near-autarky is not the right prescription. The point is illustrated strikingly by comparing Japan with Germany—another oil importer (figure 2). Germany has continued to open its markets while Japan today is more closed than it was two decades ago.

Figure 1   Asia and Japan: bilateral trade balances with the United States, 1983-92

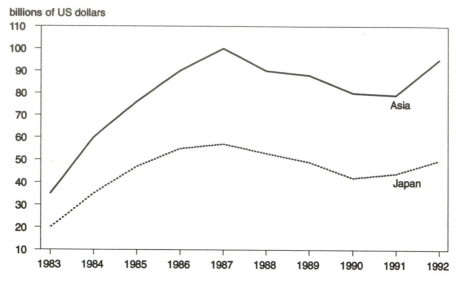

billions of US dollars

Not only the major industrial countries share this concern about Japan's openness; Korea also struggles with Japan's invisible barriers. In the case of Korea, the argument could hardly be that Korean firms don't try hard enough. Accordingly, quality and other camouflage arguments have been used to keep out Korean goods. Beyond its concern over trade access, Korea worries about the lack of technology transfer. As a relatively small economy, Korea must to a significant extent rely on the import of technology as it seeks to move up the value-added ladder, yet Japan has been uncooperative. Consequently, Korea must seek elsewhere for improved trade opportunities and also for a technology source—one more reason for it to cooperate with the United States, where technology is more readily available and increasingly cutting-edge.

Korea cannot hope on its own to make inroads into Japan. Just as Finland would not try to kick Russia around, Korea can at best play a careful game of increasing engagement with the United States to build a new relationship, no longer based on the old bonds of the Cold War era. This is all the more important because Japan has at best an ambiguous interest in fostering Korean unification. On the one hand, Japan surely wants to defuse North Korea, but on the other, it shows little enthusiasm for Korean economic and political unification.

Regional Integration

NAFTA marked a major change in US foreign trade policy. The United States traditionally had supported a multilateral, nondiscriminatory trad-

Table 1 Real effective exchange rates (1990=100)

Country	1992	1993 (January)
Japan	107.8	122.4
Korea	88.1	86.2
Malaysia	106.2	106.0
Philippines	105.5	94.8
Singapore	104.9	109.2
Taiwan	95.9	94.5
Thailand	98.3	99.4

Source: J.P. Morgan

ing system. The General Agreement on Tariffs and Trade (GATT) was the means to this end, and there was no parallel or alternative strategy. There had been a long-standing special relation with Canada, but that was so much taken for granted that it was not thought to represent a significant departure from multilateralism.

The debate about NAFTA had many overtones. Whatever their professed concerns, organized labor's chief objective was outright protectionism. But multilateralists also voiced important opposition to the regional strategy. They feared that US commitment to regional integration—Mexico first, Latin America next—would create a world of trading blocs with a concurrent weakening of GATT, GATT processes, GATT rules, and a resurgence of protectionism.

The 1993 APEC meeting and the modest plans for US-Asian collaboration that emerged must have done much to quash these fears over emerging trade blocs. However, the plans do fan fears that the United States will continue to work through non-GATT channels to improve its trade opportunities. Many US trading partners fear that the price the United States extracts for improved access to its markets will be too high. Countries that wish to control the pace and modalities of their own market opening are understandably alarmed.

The immediate reaction to an FTA proposal in many Asian economies has been rather mixed. These nations prefer a strengthened GATT and unrestricted worldwide access rather than special arrangements that come at a cost. Specifically, in a world of trade blocs, Asia could be left behind— that is, it could lose access in Europe and the United States without gaining access in the Japanese market. In an open free trade world, even players such as the United States mostly keep their gloves on. But in a narrow regional setting organized around Japan, the smaller economies could not evade a Japanese powerplay.

The APEC meeting set as an initial agenda the pursuit of framework agreements for integration of trade and services flows. That project is realistic for the larger group, but it is not the most ambitious scheme. More aggressive steps toward an FTA were resisted out of fear that they might

Table 2 Import penetration in manufacturing, 1985–90 (average percentage)

Country	Percent
Japan	5.4
US	13.3
Germany	24.6
France	27.7
Italy	21.0
Australia	23.9

Source: OECD Working Paper No. 134.

impede progress on a multilateral front. The United States, which has far more confidence in the multilateral game and its ability to play in both arenas at the same time, ought to break down this resistance by offering more exposed trading partners such as Korea entrance into an FTA of the sweepingly broad kind that NAFTA represents. In fact, the NAFTA agreement (less its last-minute compromises) ought to serve as the blueprint. There should be a provision for extension of the agreement to interested Asian economies other than Japan. Such nations would join under the same broad terms as the initial agreement.

Such a move would undoubtedly cause a lot of fuss and unrest, but for many countries, joining such a scheme is inevitable. Neither Europe nor Japan is offering deals in any credible fashion. Thus, countries will rush to sign up for the only action that is offered. The game is a bit rough, but so is the nonalignment game played by so many countries today.

Korea is a natural choice for an opening move. Its trade interests are substantial, there are plenty of pressure points (e.g., trade in services, security), and Korea is interested in a more rules-based relationship with the United States. In other words, Korea has much in common with Mexico.

For Korea, being the sparring partner of an elephant is a mixed blessing. Its strategy of paced opening with a highly centralized economic system would go overboard very rapidly during negotiations. But that may be the case in any event.

Becoming the staging ground for regional trade and development is a big gamble. It may well be what Korea needs to revive the dynamism of its past 20 years and lock in an entirely new set of opportunities at a time when its traditional advantages are exhausted by the arrival of competing economies such as China. In making such a gamble, Korea must decide whether the United States' days as a world power are coming to a close—a view not uncommon in the 1980s—or whether the United States will continue to be important, if only because there is no other power rivaling it and lots of trouble wherever one looks. The answer, without any question, is that the United States is Korea's best bet—and a good bet at that.

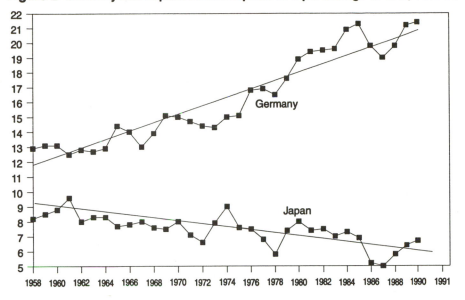

Figure 2 Germany and Japan: nonoil imports as a percentage of GNP, 1958-91

For the United States, the interest in Korea and the region is in the first place commercial. Asia is emerging as the center of the world. Increasingly, there is a perception in the United States that it may be left out of the action. Intra-Asian trade is growing by leaps and bounds, but US participation is not. An FTA is an obvious way to refocus.

US interests do go beyond the narrow issue of merchandise trade access. It is increasingly apparent that an FTA with a country that is the gateway to an entire region offers much more. There is the potential for major trade opportunities in the broadest sense in the new economic regions of Northern China, Manchuria, and Siberia. Access is more readily gained through joint ventures via Korea than may be possible from going it alone from the outside. At the same time, a trade agreement would broaden the mind, offering insight into the trade and economic culture of a region. It would highlight opportunities and consequently galvanize and channel efforts in a way that is invariably difficult for a large country such as the United States, where the home market invariably gets more attention than those abroad.

The United States needs a new and stronger mechanism to participate in regional opportunities. This is not only true for the Korean market but also for Southeast Asia, where the ties are weaker and the opportunities greater. That region in particular has resisted the notion of trade arrangements other than those reached on a multilateral basis. Also, it is coming increasingly into the Japanese sphere of influence—the immediate result of Japan's major direct investment and its accompanying market access there.

For some countries, joining an FTA as soon as possible and at any price is the obvious policy response. In the NAFTA context, that is the case for Chile and Argentina. Others—for example, Brazil—are holding off because their traditional multilateral posture obscures the view that the advantages of multilateralism may be retained without passing up the extra benefits of regionalism and letting these benefits devolve to others. But in the general context of a stampede into regionalism, even the very large economies will have to focus on regional agreements. That will be the case for Southeast Asia, just as it is in South America today.

Regional versus Global Trade

If the United States chooses to advance a regional strategy in Latin America and in Asia and succeeds, must we fear for the multilateral system? One indication comes from the rapid succession of the GATT agreement last fall on the heels of NAFTA. That is, far from resting after the politically exhausting NAFTA battle, the United States moved quickly to conclude the Uruguay Round.

Whatever lack of credibility there might have been, this determination and the success of its efforts vindicates the United States' claim to be a proponent of a multilateral system as the common denominator. Regional deals increasingly are emerging as special arrangements that allow deeper and faster forays into emerging markets rather than as a means for gaining marginal advantages in established trade relations.

It is also clear that the attention regional options get highlights the raised stakes in global negotiations. Being in a regional arrangement is good, and for many countries, it is an essential move to avoid direct discriminatory effects and, more importantly, to gain the broad, positive impacts on innovation, modernization, and inward investment. Being left out means falling behind. In that sense, regional initiatives are a powerful means for directing attention to the merits of opening and internationalization.

The China Problem

The United States has been stranded in its China policy. Having put nuclear nonproliferation and human rights at the top of the agenda and having created an unwieldy MFN process as its chief vehicle for seeking leverage on these issues, the United States both lacks success on these issues and faces the real prospect of being left out of the burgeoning Chinese market. The attempt to demonstrate flexibility in dealings with Vietnam is a good sign that economic issues can gain prominence in US-Asian relations.

Korea can help the United States in its dealing with China in two ways. First, close US-Korean cooperation, perhaps through an FTA, gives the United States more regional exposure. Second, and perhaps more importantly, Korea can help the United States gain more perspective on the human rights issue. The United States has to become more effective in human rights discussions; the best way may be increased interaction and common interests—not a jostling over MFN status. Korea could share its perspective on what progress can be made in human rights and what pressure points to use. The sheer ineffectiveness of the past decade suggests that all and any lessons other countries have learned must be welcome.

Russia in Asia

The breakup of the Soviet Union and the implosion of Russia create a totally new security situation in Asia. It is not clear what will emerge in Russia. The most dangerous situation, of course, is a strongly nationalistic, militaristic Russia that seeks to rebuild the empire. Of course, there is no risk soon since Russia is on its back. But there is another scenario that is far more interesting. Is it possible that Siberia might break away, de facto or de jure? This region offers extraordinary opportunities for an Asian-style development built around raw material resources. It has the technology, the management, and the money. The only obstacle to an ambitious program of development there is Moscow's control.

If Siberia should be opened up, a major competition will ensue. Japan would see in Siberia a long-desired resource base close to home. The issue could quickly gain major geopolitical significance. The weaker Russia becomes, the more the pressure for a better and separate deal in Siberia and the more urgent and intense the subsequent competition for access to the region. Naturally, the United States would want to be part of the action. So far, little is happening along these lines other than in oil. A much stronger focus is appropriate because this region is one of the world's most important frontiers. But beyond the narrow economic interest, the United States must also be concerned about Siberia becoming a point of conflict in Asia and about who gets the spoils. Decidedly, this is another place where a potential expansion of Japan's influence needs to be matched by a parallel US effort or better. By the same token, it is another place where US-Korean interests may run in common.

Conclusion

The United States must rethink its Asia strategy. Economic issues are paramount because the region's economic stakes are huge and economics is the driving force for regional movement. The vacuum left by the Russian collapse empties the traditional US-Japanese relationship of much of its content and calls for a new concept. US-Korean relations that have focused on very petty trade issues and financial opening need to be moved to a far more ambitious plane. Korea is the best partner for the United States to test the waters of far-reaching economic involvement in Asia.

References

Bayard, T., and S. G. Young, eds. 1989. *Economic Relations Between the United States and Korea: Conflict or Cooperation?* Washington: Institute for International Economics.

Bergsten, C. F. et al. 1993. "A New Vision for APEC." Washington: Institute for International Economics. Photocopy.

Bergsten, C. F., and M. Noland, eds. 1993a. *Pacific Dynamism and the International Economic System.* Washington: Institute for International Economics.

Bergsten, C. F., and M. Noland. 1993b. *Reconcilable Differences? United States–Japan Economic Conflict.* Washington: Institute for International Economics.

Cho Soon. 1993. *The Dynamics of Korean Economic Development.* Washington: Institute for International Economics.

Frankel, J., and M. Kahler, eds. 1993. *Regionalism and Rivalry: Japan and the United States in Pacific Asia.* Chicago: University of Chicago Press.

Kim, I., ed. 1991. *Korean Challenges and American Policy.* New York: Paragon House.

Teufel Dreyer, J., ed. 1990. *Asian-Pacific Regional Security.* Washington: The Washington Institute Press.

IV

KOREA AND THE UNITED STATES
IN THE WORLD ECONOMY

7

A Korean Perspective

KYUNG WON KIM

More than any other bilateral relationship in the world, the Korean-US relationship must be regarded as a product of the Cold War. Not only was its character shaped by imperatives of the Cold War, its very existence owed itself to the exigencies of the struggle between the United States and the Soviet Union.

When the Pacific War ended in 1945, the United States paid little attention to Korea's potential value in economic or strategic terms. Economically, Korea was seen as a country condemned to be a basket case for the indefinite future. Militarily, the Korean peninsula was regarded as a potential trap for US forces should they find themselves on it in the event of war breaking out on the Asian continent.[1]

Washington's highest priority in the Asia Pacific was Japan. Secretary of State Dean Acheson believed that the United States had to help, not obstruct, the industrial reconstruction of Japan in order to keep Japan within the Western camp, which was considered absolutely essential in the struggle against the Soviet Union.[2] US strategy, therefore, aimed at

Kyung Won Kim is Korea's former ambassador to the United States and is now president of the Institute of Social Sciences in Seoul.

1. President Harry S Truman was advised by the Joint Chiefs of Staff in a memorandum dated 25 September 1947 that "the United States has little strategic interest in maintaining the present troops and bases in Korea" and "in the event of hostilities in the Far East, our present forces in Korea would be a military liability" (Truman 1956, 325–26).

2. On Dean Acheson's views on the importance of Japan in Asia, see McGlothlen (1993).

creating a basis for long-term engagement in Japan while disengaging from Korea.

The assumptions of US strategy, however, were shattered by the North Korean military attack against South Korea in the summer of 1950. The policy of securing Japan while ceding Korea had appeared rational in terms of the relative value of Japan versus Korea. But when the Soviet and North Korean leaders decided to test US willingness to tolerate the consequences of its own strategic assumption, Washington came to embrace the Republic of Korea as an ally.

Could such an alliance survive the end of the Cold War? In a world in which there is no strategic rival to the United States, what is the glue to bind the United States and the Republic of Korea together?

Strangely enough, Korean-US relations appear to be least affected by the collapse of the Soviet Union. The North Atlantic alliance, having lost its historic raison d'etre, finds itself enmeshed in an agonizing search for a new rationale. Sino-US relations are full of highly visible strains and stresses, which used to be buried under the surface when Beijing and Washington both knew that their conspicuous display of "friendship" was aimed at those watching in Moscow. Between Tokyo and Washington, only strong economic and geopolitical interdependence keep the talk in Japan of that country becoming a "normal" (i.e., armed) state and the United States' Japan bashing within bounds. Clearly, the disappearance of the Soviet Union as a common threat has made relations among yesterday's allies—although they are still friends—a great deal more complicated than before.

One reason for the exceptional continuity in Korean-American relations must have to do with the continuing intransigence of the North Korean regime. On the Korean peninsula, the Cold War clock still ticks. If anything, the threat posed by North Korea's suspected nuclear weapons program seems to have infused new energy into the Seoul-Washington connection, as demonstrated in President Clinton's repeated expressions of US commitment to the security of South Korea. Seoul and Washington have a common agenda and a definite need to stand together. The decision to suspend phased reduction of US troops stationed in South Korea is explicitly in response to North Korean nuclear intransigence.

Despite the apparent continuity of the alliance, however, we must think beyond the current situation and ask the question: with the glue of anti-communism gone, what are the common strategic interests that can keep Korea and the United States working together in the post–Cold War world?

New Challenges to US Leadership

The decline and fall of the Soviet Union has left the United States as the only world superpower. It was, therefore, not altogether unreasonable for the American president (President Bush in this instance) to predict the birth of a "new international order," presumably incorporating America's preferred principles of market economy and political democracy. Philosophically, it was claimed that history had come to its end because there was no longer any viable alternative to liberal democracy (Fukuyama 1989, 3–18). Many believed that American ideas as well as American power had triumphed.

But the geopolitical and philosophical triumph of the United States coincided with severe domestic distress. The state of the US economy, along with a host of other domestic ills, raised doubts about the future viability of the United States as the only superpower. What made this future even more uncertain was that the relative economic decline of the United States occurred as Europe and Japan reached economic ascendence. More recently, Europe and Japan have been mired in widely advertised economic ills of their own. But the long-term challenge they pose to US economic supremacy is as real as it was when the Soviet empire fell apart.

China, too, presents a potential threat to US leadership (Kristof 1993, 59–74). China's conversion to a market economy is a welcome development from the United States' viewpoint. But the dynamic growth released by this conversion confronts the United States with the possibility that sometime in the next century China may well overtake the United States as the world's largest economy. Even then, individual Chinese will be by far poorer than Americans. But the ability to purchase military power depends on the gross size of the national income rather than the national income per individual. In other words, China may well be in a position to challenge US leadership, at least in East Asia if not throughout the world.

China's intentions are, however, difficult to read. Some observers have called attention to China's weapons modernization program, which seems to include a plan to acquire carriers for its navy, as well as new, more advanced fighters for its air force. But as yet, it is hard to be convinced that China is building military force for the purpose of challenging US military supremacy.

Despite the currently limited character of China's military modernization program, it is significant that power is shifting from the West to the East for the first time in modern history. For about 500 years, the trend has been in the other direction. Ever since the Western powers humbled China in the 19th century, the possibility that China could become an equal, if not superior, power demanding appropriate treatment was never seriously entertained by Western statesmen. The rise of China, therefore, presents Western powers with a fundamental psychological problem—that is, envisaging a world order that accommodates China as a truly equal power.

Russia presents another challenge. The current US attitude toward Russia reminds one of past US attitudes toward Germany and Japan. There seems to be an innate US tendency to be kind to those it has defeated in battle. Particularly, those who surrender unconditionally and promise to embrace the American creed are forgiven instantly and helped generously. The problem in Russia's case, however, is that President Boris Yeltsin seems to be having second thoughts about his earlier promise to adopt American-style democracy and its economic system. Economic reform is being slowed if not wholly abandoned; politically, the idea of a liberal democratic Russia must now be seen for what it always has been—an idea, not a reality.

The ambiguity of the Russian situation leads to ambiguity in the US policy toward it. Just as there is a lack of clarity about Eastern Europe's relationship to NATO, it is far from clear whether Russia should be regarded as a potential threat to the West or as a contributor to the stability of the global balance of power.

In the post–Cold War world, the United States faces several potential rivals rather than one known rival.[3] The bipolar world was more dangerous, but the postbipolar world is more complicated. The goal of the Cold War was to contain one known enemy. But in the post–Cold War world, it is not enough for the United States to restrain one single, identifiable power. The United States must be able to restrain any and all potential superpowers—former allies as well as former adversaries. It is for this reason that the Pentagon report, *Defense Planning Guidance for the Fiscal Years 1994–1999*, must be regarded as a document reflective of America's fundamental strategic interests, even though it was officially disavowed following a *New York Times* report on it. It states that to prevent other states from challenging US leadership, the United States "must maintain the mechanisms for deterring potential competitors from even aspiring to a larger regional or global role." The official disavowal must have had less to do with the substance of the argument than with the embarrassment caused by the rare candor with which the Pentagon report laid bare the logic of America's post–Cold War strategic requirement. In fact, official speeches by President Bill Clinton, Secretary of State Warren Christopher, and National Security Adviser Anthony Lake do nothing to repudiate the strategic concept made explicit in the Pentagon report. On the contrary, official pronouncements on US foreign policy show that, contrary to Under Secretary of State Peter Tarnoff's widely reported reflections on the need to reduce US involvement in the world, the United States is not about to reduce its commitments abroad and disengage from the world. All of the alliances originally created to meet the Soviet challenge are still there and show no signs of being discontinued. All of America's avowed commitments have been reconfirmed and remain intact. If anything, US foreign policy seems to have become more activist than before. No longer

---

3. For an interesting speculative essay on the shape of the future world order, with especially stimulating comments on the meaning of "the most indisputably upwardly-mobile China," see *The Economist*, 8–14 January 1994, 19–21.

preoccupied with containing communism, Washington seeks to spread free markets and political democracy. Human rights has returned to the center of the US foreign policy agenda with greater vigor because the nations the United States targets feel more vulnerable to pressure that is unchecked by a rival superpower.

Goals of a US Strategy

Whoever is in the White House, US strategy in the post–Cold War world must be guided by five global goals. First, the primary goal of US foreign policy must be to protect the US leadership role. Without it, no other objective can be safe. Smaller powers can achieve their national interests without aiming at primacy in the world. But a nation with the largest economy and the most powerful military must avoid erosion of its leadership and the consequent challenges to this role by potential rivals. Washington cannot concede leadership in one area and expect to exercise it effectively in another area. To be sure, the United States can and often must share the burden of leadership with other nations. But burden sharing must also be US-led and is not a substitute for that leadership.

Second, in order to protect its leadership role, the United States must see to it that a balance of power is maintained globally—that is, between Europe, Russia, and East Asia—and regionally within Europe and East Asia. The necessity for equilibrium is axiomatic. It is the first principle of geopolitics.

A global balance of power will remain the natural condition of the world for the foreseeable future. Neither Europe nor East Asia is about to overwhelm the other. Nor are they likely to embrace each other in a grand global alliance against the United States. On the contrary, East Asia is likely to remain more oriented toward North America than Europe, as shown by the embryonic Asia Pacific Economic Cooperation (APEC) effort. The United States, however, must remain focused on Russia as well. Radical collapse of political authority in Russia may tempt China into territorial (irredentist) adventurism. It will be equally important to guide Russia away from resurrecting the traditional expansionism of pan-Slavic nationalism.

The regional balance of power within Europe will continue to rest on Germany's self-restraint. For the moment, problems arising out of unification are fully absorbing the energies of the German people. But the strength inherent in the German nation, together with the fragility of the Balkan states and the historical inclinations of many central European nations to coalesce around Germany, makes the future role of Germany within Europe a little more problematic than is assumed by many. It is because of this German problem that the United States welcomes European integration, although a single Europe with common foreign and security policy would also complicate the Atlantic relationship.

It is in East Asia that the United States finds the task of balancing power most complex. Basically, East Asia contains one former superpower still falling apart, one future superpower rising fast, and one potential superpower unsure of its identity. There is a balance of power, but it is one with tremendous dynamism built into it. Transformation in East Asia today is nothing short of revolutionary. Modernization of traditional societies and the political change and democratization subsequent to it in many cases, together with tectonic shifts in the balance of power, are producing a wholly new political landscape in the world's most populous region.

To protect its leadership role in the region, the United States must neither greatly antagonize China and Japan nor exploit the "natural" rivalry between China and Japan to the point of endangering the peace and stability of the region. To make the first mistake, US policymakers would have to be incredibly incompetent. But the second possibility can come to pass without the United States making a major blunder. The level of trust between Beijing and Tokyo cannot be presumed to be high. And both are proud, ambitious nations. The only thing that is keeping them from pushing each other into an arms race is Japan's acceptance of the US security commitment as a substitute for building a military force of its own that would be commensurate with its economic power. The United States therefore needs to stay in East Asia, continuing to provide a credible security umbrella for Japan, without which a dialectic of mutual distrust may easily generate an acute arms race between Asia's two most powerful nations.

Third, in a little longer perspective, spreading free markets and democracy is ultimately the most enduring way to protect US interests. Geopolitical equilibrium is a necessity. But it is inherently an unstable device because, given the dynamism of economic growth and the dialectic of mutual distrust, a balance of power can never be more than transitory.

Ultimately, nation-states need to be protected against their own worst instincts. Although there is no proven way to accomplish this, history so far shows that states under the control of self-governing people are least inclined to go to war against each other. Promoting market economy and political democracy, seen in this perspective, becomes the ultimate security policy.

But there are almost insurmountable constraints on the effectiveness of a policy promoting democracy. As can be seen in the experience of US diplomacy, the means employed to promote democracy are either irrelevant, counterproductive, or at best marginally effective. Historically, there is no evidence to suggest that American efforts in this direction have transformed a single state from authoritarian into democratic rule. The examples of Germany and Japan are not relevant unless one is prepared to argue that the United States should go to war to bring about democratic conversion. Recent trends toward democratization in Korea and Taiwan have far more to do with domestic evolution than external trauma.[4] Democratic conversion in Central European states, too, was a product of their own history, while the difficulties encountered in Russia cannot be helped away by the good intentions of the Western powers. That China's political modernization will have to be negotiated by the balance of China's own domestic forces is obvious, except to those who refuse to recognize the weight of history. In any case, America's desire to see the "enlargement" of market economy and political democracy is both understandable and troublesome. The pursuit of this goal will require American policymakers to develop greater appreciation of the intractability of history and a willingness to balance what is desirable with what is possible.

America's fourth objective is to prevent the spread of weapons of mass destruction among nations that do not possess them already. The rationale for this policy is to prevent regional as opposed to global conflicts. From the perspective of middle powers, however, the distinction between global and regional conflict is academic. For a regional power, a regional war is total war. A revisionist power committed to bringing about change in the regional hierarchy of power will not see any moral reason to refrain from acquiring weapons of mass destruction.

It is precisely for this reason that the United States must oppose acquisition of weapons of mass destruction by regional powers. The United States, in other words, equates international stability with maintenance of the existing regional hierarchy of power it sponsors. The spread of nuclear weapons and smart weapons is essentially a political problem—a textbook example of the struggle for power between status quo and revisionist states.

The United States, however, cannot openly acknowledge the political nature of the problem. Instead, Washington defines the problem as a legal-technical one. But if this is the case—that the problem is a matter of arriving at a universal legal norm—there are obvious inconsistencies: Israel, India, and Pakistan, for example. Caught between the legal pretense and the political character of the issue, the United States tends to lack consistency of approach, instead experimenting with a variety of means, including the rhetoric of single-issue pressure tactics, tit-for-tat bargaining, and even downright bribery, as in the cases of Ukraine and North Korea.

Finally, on the economic plane, the current US strategy sharply contrasts with the approach adopted following World War II. While the United States, confident of its margin of economic superiority, created multilateral institutions such as the International Bank for Reconstruction and

---

4. For the author's views on democratization of authoritarian regimes, see Kyung-won Kim (1993, 11–25).

Development, the International Monetary Fund, and the General Agreement on Tariffs and Trade (GATT) during the 1940s, it is now resorting to simultaneous multilateral, regional, and bilateral approaches. The chief reason for adopting multiple approaches is to maximize the opportunities for protecting US economic interests. Creation of the Bretton Woods system was hardly an act of altruism either. But as the Cold War unfolded, the United States had to display a certain degree of generosity to the nations it wanted to keep on its side of the Iron Curtain. Fortunately for the West, the US margin of economic superiority was wide enough to allow geopolitical considerations to define the strategic framework for its international economic policies.

In the 1990s, however, the United States has neither the need nor the margin of superiority to continue the kind of economic leadership it once exercised. Forcing the inclusion of agricultural products as well as financial services and intellectual property rights within a strengthened GATT regime was not enough to prevent the United States from reacting to rising European regionalism with its own North American regional approach. As for APEC, whatever its future potential, it has as yet no operative substance. In the meantime, the United States is quite aware that neither the post–Uruguay Round GATT nor the North American Free Trade Agreement (NAFTA) is going to resolve the single most important geoeconomic problem: namely, the trade disequilibrium with Japan. There is also the prospect of an even greater trade deficit with China in the not-too-distant future. It is therefore easy to understand why the United States continues to resort to bilateral trade negotiations as well as making use of regional and global possibilities.

There are problems with this approach, however. First, negotiations in this context are easily seen as a sign of economic weakness rather than strength. Bilateral trade negotiations essentially bypass multilateral trade dispute settlement procedures, and point up the degree to which America's negotiating strategy is based on an implicit linkage between economic and geopolitical interests. This in the short run can often produce desired results, at least on paper, but in the long run risks forcing the trading partner to reformulate basic assumptions about the balance between economic and geopolitical interests. Trade friction beyond a certain point may not be worth enduring, depending on the trading partners' subjective view of the geopolitical stakes for whose sake trade friction has been tolerated.

The end of the Cold War has elevated the United States to a historically unparalleled height in its power and prestige. Truly, *pax Americana*, a notion more often cited by America's critics than its defenders in the past, has become a reality. Yet history shows that fulfillment of an ambition often exhausts the energy used to achieve it and the sense of purpose is lost. This is not the case with the United States today. But in the new global context, the country's need to redefine its goals is nonetheless real and urgent. Without a clear definition of US interests and objectives, there is no way to differentiate between challenges that must be faced and problems that seem serious because they defy easy solution. The problems of Bosnia, Somalia, and Haiti hardly define America's global goals. Redefining relations with Europe, Japan, China, and Russia constitutes the real agenda facing the United States today.

How Korea Fits In

Is Korea in a category with Bosnia, Somalia, and Haiti or one with Europe, Japan, China, and Russia? To a large extent, the answer will depend upon Korea's own conception of its strategic objectives, as well as America's geopolitical goals. Are Korea's geopolitical interests consistent with American interests? Even to raise a question such as this must seem strange to those who have been actively engaged in managing the Cold War strategies. It used to be left to revisionist historians to ask even such basic questions as the extent to which Korean interests coincided and in what areas they diverged.

National Security

Korea's foremost strategic necessity is survival. Unlike the United States, Korea has no "global" goal that is essential to its own vital interests and that lies within the range of the obtainable.

The necessity for survival transcends the condition of national division, for it is rooted in the geopolitical reality of Korea. For decades now, Korea's survival has tended to be equated with survival against the threat from North Korea. The entire security framework, including the US military component, was understood within the context of the North-South conflict.

The end of the Cold War, however, makes it necessary to examine the problem of survival for a postdivision Korea as well. Historically, protecting the political independence of Korea has never been easy. Securing political autonomy for Korea was as difficult before as it was after the division.

Korea's security dilemma is inherent in the disequilibrium of resources. However successful Korea becomes in gaining national strength, it will never gain the physical strength that would provide it political security. Its neighbors are too large for Korea to be able to purchase political independence through military might.

The essence of the Korean problem has been that Korea has not been strong enough to assure its neighbors that the peninsula would not fall under the domination of one of them. The incentive for its neighbors to strike preemptively was inherent in the radical disequilibrium of power. Therefore, Korea needs two things: military capacity sufficient to discourage all potential enemies from aggression and a diplomacy that convinces Korea's neighbors of its intent to maintain continued autonomy.

Unification

Another objective of paramount importance to the Korean nation is reunification. This is not only a matter of national sentiment but also a geopolitical requirement. Without unification, survival will always be much more difficult to secure.

Unification requires two conditions. First, Korea must convince its neighbors that unification is consistent with their geopolitical interests. Second, this must occur within the context of a North Korean political change of structural proportions.

The first requirement has been more or less fulfilled through changes within the former Soviet Union and the People's Republic of China. Although Beijing continues to maintain cordial and relatively close relations with North Korea, it is doubtful that China would be either able or willing to intervene in internal Korean affairs to prevent unification. As for Russia, the West is worried over the rise of extreme nationalism and the growing assertiveness in Moscow's foreign policy behavior. But it is not clear that Russian nationalism would favor North Korea against the prospect of a united Korea, which would have no inherent conflict of interest with Russia. Korea's relations with Japan remain complex. But mutual interdependence has been growing steadily, and postwar generations in both nations are becoming increasingly capable of managing their relations with pragmatism and common sense.

The majority of the Korean people certainly do not harbor any illusion that their immediate neighbors share their deep longing for unification. If enthusiasm for Korean unification is somewhat limited outside Korea, it is only to be expected. What is new in the post–Cold War era, however, is that no major power actively opposes unification of Korea. The great remaining challenge for Korean diplomacy is to develop a sense of balance and an instinctive appreciation of nuance, both qualities that were not in prominent display during the Cold War period; these qualities are necessary to win support for unification from the major powers. If lucidity and loyalty characterized the diplomacy of the bipolar world, Korea's diplomacy must henceforth demonstrate that it can also manage complexity and rationality.

Internal conditions in North Korea must be considered ripe for change. The economy, which was not exactly vigorous to begin with, has been deteriorating rapidly since the trade partners of the old Council for Mutual Economic Assistance all deserted the socialist ways of conducting economic relations. To say that North Korea is diplomatically isolated does not even begin to convey the trauma North Korea's leaders must have experienced when they lost all their ideological allies. Not only the loneliness of being abandoned by all of its allies, but the philosophical bewilderment in the face of the sudden and totally unanticipated collapse of communism must have gnawed at North Korean leaders' innermost faith while forcing them tactically to further harden their external stance. Suddenly or gradually, the North Korean system cannot but change.

Most South Koreans confess that they dread the consequences of North Korea's sudden collapse. The official position of the government of the Republic of Korea is to agree with the North Korean government's rejection of "unification by absorption." But South Korea cannot decide whether change in North Korea is going to be dramatic or prosaic. North Korea's future will be decided by "internal contradictions" within North Korea. South Korea must be prepared to deal with either contingency.

Regional Security Arrangement

Korea's regional goal is to play a constructive role in building a new architecture for a stable security equilibrium. As stressed before, Korea needs to be part of a system based on a balance of power, not a system with a hegemon. Its survival and unification depend upon cooperative relationships with all its neighbors. These requirements all suggest that, from Korea's point of view, it is best to build a multilateral regional framework.

The obstacles to such an arrangement are considerable. To begin with, Northeast Asia is in a period of transition. The rise of China, political reform in Japan, continuing confusion in Russia, industrialization and democratization in South Korea, and anticipated change in North Korea make Northeast Asia a region of dynamic change, not an area of stable balance. Second, the region lacks the tradition of multilateral diplomacy. The traditional East Asian system was an openly hierarchical one, while multilateralism requires the appearance (if not the actuality) of equality. Third, there are a number of unresolved territorial disputes between Russia and Japan, Russia and China, and between China and many others.

Yet these obstacles make a new security architecture all the more necessary. In a period of dynamic change, shifts in the power balance need to be accepted as such and incorporated into a legitimate institutional framework. It makes no sense to leave China out in the cold. Nor does it make sense to accord China a new status without persuading it to accept new responsibilities. China's military modernization must be accompanied by greater transparency in a regional institutional setting.

Can Korea play a meaningful role in building toward that regional architecture? The project will be enormously difficult. Neither the Association of Southeast Asian Nations (ASEAN) regional security forum nor an Asian version of the Conference on Security and Cooperation in Europe (CSCE) will meet North Asia's special needs; the job of constructing a House of Northeast Asia must begin with the realities in the region itself and not some abstract model borrowed from elsewhere.

The most fundamental reality in Northeast Asia is that the power equilibrium has been and continues to be predicated upon US participation in the region's security system. Briefly, US military presence allows Japan to refrain from acquiring a military capability commensurate with its economic power and consistent with the need to defend its vital interests. To the extent that a new security architecture for Northeast Asia must begin by building upon this reality, Korea's role must be understood in the context of Korea's military ties to the United States.

Korean-US security ties are accepted on both sides in the context of the North Korean threat. How the relationship can be politically redefined in the postunification context, and particularly in relation to the need for a new regional security architecture, will constitute the major foreign policy challenge to Korean statesmen in the post–Cold War era.

Nuclear Weapons

Another external goal of Korea's must be to prevent the unregulated spread of weapons of mass destruction. This is a particularly acute problem for Korea because of North Korea's reported nuclear weapons ambition. But it must also be admitted that Korean and US interests are not completely coextensive. Both Seoul and Washington definitely oppose North Koreans acquiring nuclear weapons. But the primary US concern is to protect the integrity of the Non-Proliferation Treaty (NPT) regime, whereas Korea's interest is much closer to home. Consequently, the United States is prepared to go to great lengths to stop the North Koreans from developing, producing, and deploying nuclear weapons. South Korea, on the other hand, must be more concerned with what weapons North Korea may already possess because current inventory will have a more immediate impact on Korean security than production. In other words, the United States may focus upon North Korea's acceptance of regular inspections by the International Atomic Energy Agency (IAEA), while South Korea must insist on more intrusive inspection.

Another gap between US and Korean interests is that while the United States must regard South Korea as a potential N+1 country whose potential nuclear ambition must be checked as much as North Korea's, the South Korean public tends to see President Roh Tae Woo's permanent renunciation of plutonium technology as a decision the United States forced upon Korea to limit its "nuclear sovereignty." Particularly if the United States fails to persuade North Korea to guarantee complete and unhindered transparency, the South Korean government will come under growing domestic pressure to reconsider its nuclear policy.

Korean Trade Policy

Finally, on trade issues, Korea prefers a global, multilateral regime. To be sure, the new GATT rules are already generating substantial political heat. Protest by groups affected most by the new rules, such as farmers, have often been violent and will not be assuaged easily.

But from the perspective of a middle power, it is by far preferable to rely on a universal system of trade rules rather than being subject to bilateral political pressure for trade concessions from a major trading nation with which it faces unequal geopolitical and economic stakes. In practice, however, a middle power has very little leverage for choosing between multilateral, regional, and bilateral approaches.

For Korea, regionalism raises awkward questions. While watching the rise of regionalism in Europe and North America helplessly, it must participate in the APEC process, knowing full well that it is in no way equivalent to the other regional institutions. Not being a member of ASEAN, Korea has hesitated to endorse the East Asian Economic Caucus (EAEC) proposed by Malaysian Prime Minister Mahatir. But with the formal launching of NAFTA, there is no longer any rationale to oppose the formation of the EAEC. Australia and New Zealand, non-NAFTA members of the APEC, should be invited to join the EAEC.

Ultimately, Korea's natural economic territory (NET), a concept proposed by Robert Scalapino, is likely to comprise Japan, Northeast China, and Far Eastern Russia. This is a region where obstacles to economic integration have been fast disappearing, leading to rapid trade and investment growth.

What geopolitical impact Northeast Asian economic integration will have is difficult to foresee. Growing economic interdependence will certainly reduce political tensions. The vast pool of technology, capital, and natural and human resources will make the region one of the most dynamic NETs. Whether and to what degree Northeast Asian regionalism will tend to diminish the importance of the United States in the region's affairs is difficult to predict confidently. No matter what one may think of various developmental possibilities, it is important not to fall into the trap of thinking that Northeast Asian integration is going to create a civilizational alliance *a la* Samuel Huntington (1993, 22–49). Such a vision ignores too many of history's imponderables and complexities.

A brief look at the geopolitical and economic goals of Korea and the United States reveals that there are areas in which Korean and American interests largely coincide, as well as those in which there are likely to be varying degrees of tension. Post–Cold War relations will be more complicated and, it is hoped, more rewarding in the long run.[5]

There is an important area in which interests coincide: a hegemonic order in East Asia would threaten US leadership as well as the political independence of Korea. This coincidence of vital strategic interests makes Korea's position unique among East Asian nations. But coincidence of interests does not guarantee policy coordination. Geopolitical realities were not fundamentally different at the turn of the century or in the post–World War II period. Yet there was no entente between Seoul and Washington. On the contrary, US policy in both periods tended to be obsessed with larger regional powers. In the eyes of US policymakers, Korea was too small to matter.[6]

American critics of the US foreign policy tradition often point to its bouts of isolationism. But Thomas Jefferson's advice to enter into "entangling alliances with none," often wrongly attributed to George Washington, is not an exhortation to isolationism. Rather, unilateral intervention, which leads to no "entangling" alliances but which may be mounted in defense of Jefferson's other "global goals" of "peace, commerce, and honest friendship," is a recurring pattern in America's external behavior. What the United States lacks is not the willingness to intervene; rather, it is the habit of measured involvement that is missing in traditional US foreign policy.

America's geopolitical reality demands a balance of power in Europe and in East Asia. But the United States is not in the habit of calibrating tremors in the power equilibrium, and it consequently tends to react to a crisis rather than to try to create a structure to prevent it. Furthermore, since the United States tends to understand balance of power in physical-quantitative terms, it pays little attention to the dynamics of interrelationships among the regional states, a tendency in sharp contrast to the British understanding of balance of power, which encompasses developments in the smaller states of a region.

As for the Korean tradition, both history and geography have combined to shape Korea's external relations in a pattern of unipolar alliance. Having neither the means nor the cultural tradition of balancing off foreign powers, Korea's relations with the outside world moved from Sinocentric to Japanese colonial rule to the Cold War alliance with the United States. It is only recently, with the end of the Cold War, that the need to shape its external relations in a polycentric fashion has been thrust upon the Korean

---

5. For the author's views on the more rewarding dimensions of post–Cold War Korean-US relations, see Kim (1990, 231–52).

6. Even today, those who try to assure Koreans of America's interest point to the fact that, as a newly industrializing economy, Korea is no longer that small. What they fail to point out is that Korea will always be comparatively small in its geopolitical context.

people. But because the equilibrium most conducive to Korean political autonomy is one based on the continued US participation in the East Asian security system, Korea would no doubt continue to prefer to manage the regional equilibrium in an alliance with the United States. Whether this will actually be the case will depend on US attitudes, not on Korea's choice.

The consequences of the United States distancing itself from the East Asian security setting are not straightforward. Unstable rivalry, regional condominium, or possibly a creative regional architecture are some of the possibilities. Korea's role in these scenarios will be to search for a place within the emerging geopolitical framework that provides the best insurance for its political independence. Whatever form such a strategy may take, if the United States drifts away from East Asia, Korea will have no choice but to identify its position in relation to a newly emerging Asian power. But this is a possibility only if the United States ignores the fundamental coincidence of geopolitical interests between Korea and the United States. The task of statesmen in both nations will be to make certain that strategic policies do not diverge from this complementarity of interests.

Once this central axiom is understood, it should be relatively easy to manage cooperative strategies to support US leadership and Korean autonomy and unification. Korea's participation in the Gulf War, antiterrorism efforts, and the global economic and environmental agenda are all consistent with US leadership. By the same token, the US security commitment to South Korea is manifested in efforts to persuade North Korea to renounce nuclear weapons and support for peaceful unification.

One issue on which there could be a difference of emphasis is the North Korean nuclear problem. This difference of emphasis may arise because the practical consequences of the different scenarios mentioned above will affect Korea and the United States somewhat differently. But, here again, if policymakers are able to concentrate on the central, shared goal, there need not be serious differences. The so-called gap between hard-liners and soft-liners is not so much a conflict between two contradictory policies as a matter of setting a tactical time frame in which there has to be a continuum of negotiations and sanctions. Negotiated settlement is not likely without the threat of sanctions, and the purpose of threatening sanctions is to bring about negotiated solution.

Conclusion

The United States needs to think seriously about the long-term implications of its current approach. Resorting to multiple approaches may seem justified by the arithmetic of more is more. But without a coherent architectural blueprint, more can simply lead to more confusion. How does the United States see NAFTA in relation to the APEC? If the latter develops into a structure for internal trade liberalization, as NAFTA is assumed to do, how will other nations view the position of the United States, which will not only enjoy dual membership but be in a position to play *divide et impera* against other member states? Add bilateral pressure tactics, and all attempts at multilateralism will be seen as mere pretense.

In the end, the post–Cold War relationship between Korea and the United States will depend on how the United States responds to the challenge of being the greatest economic and military power in a highly dynamic and volatile world. Will the United States proceed from a clearly defined place and play its role accordingly? Or will the United States continue to respond with knee-jerk reactions to unfolding events?

Preaching cooperation will make little difference. It will be even more futile to evoke the "good old days" of the Cold War era. Only a clear conception of goals and interests will make it possible for Korea and the United States to work together in the new post–Cold War world.

References

Fukuyama, Francis. 1989. "The End of History." *The National Interest* no. 16 (Summer): 3–18.

Huntington, Samuel P. 1993. "The Clash of Civilizations?" *Foreign Affairs* 72, no. 3 (Summer): 22–49.

Kim, Kyung Won. 1990. "Beyond the Cold War: The Future of Korea-US Relations." In Robert Sutter and Han Sungjoo, *Korea-U.S. Relations in a Changing World*. Berkeley, CA: Institute of East Asian Studies Press, University of California.

Kim, Kyung Won. 1993. "Marx, Schumpeter, and the East Asian Experience." In Larry Diamond and Marc F. Plattner, *Capitalism, Socialism, and Democracy Revisited*. Baltimore: The Johns Hopkins University Press.

Kristof, Nicholas D. 1993. "The Rise of China." *Foreign Affairs* (November/December): 59–74.

McGlothlen, Donald L. 1993. *Controlling the Waves: Dean Acheson and U.S. Foreign Policy in Asia*. New York: Norton.

Truman, Harry S. 1956. *Memoirs by Harry S Truman: Years of Trial and Hope, 1946–1952*. Garden City, NY: Doubleday & Company.

8

An American Perspective

ROBERT ZOELLICK

A. C. Nahm opens his history of Korea by explaining that Korea is known in the West as "the Land of the Morning Calm" (1988, 17). Very few Americans would recognize that appellation. Instead, Korea evokes other images: a grim and savage war in a raw land where the Cold War turned red hot; a television show, M.A.S.H., that was a comedy of irony, folly, and escape amidst a bewildering siege that no one seemed to win; and a society and economy that seems forbidding, where Chrysler's mid-priced K car was alleged in America's 1988 election campaign to cost a whopping $48,000. These visions of Korea are associated with a slightly more commonly recognized name: the Hermit Kingdom.

The reality of Korea over the past 40 years presents still another picture. Korea is an incredible success story of the Cold War era. Politically, it moved from oppressive colonial rule to a sharp partition, then through a terribly destructive war, authoritarian and military governments, and onto political liberalization, democracy, and a peaceful transition of government after free elections. Economically, Korea forged an outward-looking development strategy, spurring an annual average growth rate in real terms of nearly 9 percent from 1962 to 1991. The nation overcame extreme poverty and widespread unemployment. It managed an extraordinary foreign debt (almost $47 billion, or over 52 percent of GNP, in 1991). In 1991, the Republic of Korea, poor in resources and with a territory about the size of Indiana, was the 11th largest trading nation in the world (SaKong 1993, 10, table A.35, 14, and 20).

Robert Zoellick is former undersecretary of state for economics and White House deputy chief of staff and is currently executive vice president and general counsel at Fannie Mae.

Indeed, Korea is one of the first nations from the developing world to have created an economy that warrants treatment as one of the industrialized, developed nations. In 1992, US merchandise exports to Korea ($14.6 billion) slightly exceeded US exports to France.[1] Korea's incredible climb makes it a potential model for others and the proud subject of review in the World Bank's 1993 report *The East Asian Miracle*.

The Republic of Korea also has moved forward as a world citizen and a player on the political stage. In 1988, Korea successfully hosted the 24th Olympiad. In 1991, the Asia Pacific Economic Cooperation meeting was held in Seoul, where participants agreed on the admission of China, Taiwan, and Hong Kong into this evolving regional group, a result achieved in notable part through Korean labors. In 1991 and 1992, Korea achieved its long-sought goals of recognition by China and the then–Soviet Union, and admission to the United Nations. During the Gulf War, Korea made a financial contribution to the US-led effort to reverse Iraq's aggression against Kuwait, the first major United Nations effort of its kind since the Korean War.

Indeed, in some respects, Korea is better positioned than many nations to transform its outward-oriented economic strategy into a broader agenda of engagement—especially with the United States. At the geopolitical level, Korea has a large, modern military capability that is the bedrock of its own defense and that might over time become a contributor to a wider, collective security effort. Unlike Japan, Korea does not confront claims that it is a security "free rider" or a debate over whether it should have a strong military. In fact, Korean forces fought with the United States and South Vietnam during the Vietnam War.

At the human relations level, Korea also has some special assets. Korean immigrants to the United States are valued contributors to American society and form cohesive communities in some large US cities; they enrich national bilateral ties. A large number of Koreans attend graduate schools in the United States, and many obtain advanced degrees before returning to Korea, establishing a lettered link between the two countries. Similarly, a large percentage of the Korean public is Christian, forging a bond of faith for millions of citizens of both nations who might not otherwise have much interest in international relations.[2]

Today, Korea lies on the fault line, literally and figuratively, between the promise and dangers of the post–Cold War era. Koreans have accomplished astounding results in a relatively short time. But success creates new responsibilities for Korea within the global system, which enabled it first to survive and then to thrive.

---

1. US Department of Commerce News, "United States Merchandise Trade: 1992 Final Report," (12 May 1993), Exhibit 11, p. 16.

2. See Nahm (1988, 500–02) for statistics on religious denominations.

That global system is itself in flux. The system's primary architect, the United States, is reevaluating its goals, capabilities, interests, and even relationships. Korea obviously has an enormous interest in the outcome of these equations. It is the historic land bridge between the Asian mainland and Japan. Korea's big neighbors—Japan, China, and Russia—are all struggling through their own political and economic transformations. And the Republic of Korea shares the peninsula with a dangerous, isolated regime that has been seeking nuclear weapons and missiles to deliver them. Furthermore, to continue its economic progress, Korea needs open markets abroad and foreign investments and technology at home to enable its economy to be competitive in higher value-added sectors.

Within this context, Korea should be exceedingly interested in encouraging ongoing, or even stronger, American interest in Korea. This engagement should be broad-based—political, economic, security, and cultural. And to sustain these ties, Korean government and opinion leaders will need to help the Korean public recognize that they now have global and regional responsibilities. In other words, Korea has the difficult task of developing a sense of its place in the world, a consciousness that matches its remarkable internal changes.

To address American and Korean global goals in this post–Cold War era, this paper will consider the United States in the Post–Cold War world, Korea at the launch of the post–Cold War world, and a US-Korean agenda.

The United States in the Post–Cold War World

In the years following World War II, the United States developed a strategy to guide its global engagement. While containment of communism became the guiding principle, the strategy depended on a number of complementary components. These elements included the reconstruction of Western Europe and Japan, the establishment of international institutions and regimes that encouraged trade and capital flows, decolonization and development, and a network of security alliances, with the United States at the hub of each. The core US objective was to promote Western Europe and Japan as partners as well as allies against communist threats and thus provide a model from the so-called Third World in the contest against the Second World. The United States also would foster an international system that offered opportunities for the developing nations to help themselves. It helped create new structures—such as the North Atlantic Treaty Organization (NATO), the European Community, the World Bank and the International Monetary Fund (IMF), the General Agreement on Tariffs and Trade (GATT), the US-Japan Security Treaty, and the Southeast Asia Treaty Organization—through which it pursued this strategy.

With the end of the Cold War, the United States should have two similar strategic objectives. First, it must maintain strong ties with Western Europe and Japan, its primary economic, security, and political partners. It cannot take these relationships for granted. In the absence of the glue of an omnipresent and obvious security threat, the competition, contrasts, and even conflicts among the three could lead to acrimony or alienation. In effect, there needs to be an overhaul in the old Cold War structures to address a new generation of challenges.

The second objective should be to extend these structures to incorporate new partners. These are the nations, such as Korea, that have been building market economies with pluralistic and evolving democratic political systems. This group includes many nations in East Asia, Latin America, Central and Eastern Europe, and perhaps some day Russia. The United States has a common interest in their success, just as 45 years ago the United States perceived strategic advantage in the prosperity of a peaceful, democratic Japan and Western Europe. Now these potential partners must be better integrated into global and regional structures that recognize both mutual benefits and responsibilities.

Over the past few years, the United States has been developing these new structures of its post–Cold War engagement. In some cases, it has been trying to adjust existing arrangements to meet new needs. For example, to meet new demands, the United States has worked to modify NATO's force posture, integrated command structures, political consultations, and perhaps even membership. The Uruguay Round of the GATT is in effect another such adaptation; it expands coverage in such areas as intellectual property, agriculture, and services; improves the dispute resolution machinery; and seeks to phase out discrimination that favored developing economies, which now need to share systemic duties.

The United States has also tried to create new structures to enhance integration and cooperation with its new partners, especially in Latin America and East Asia. The North American Free Trade Agreement, or NAFTA, is a good example of an economic structure that could be the cornerstone of closer cooperation across a broad agenda. Similarly, the Enterprise for the Americas Initiative (EAI) sought to expand US economic cooperation—through reduction of official debt, environmental action funded through the debt relief, investment reforms, and trade facilitation agreements leading to free trade agreements—and thus to lend momentum to an impressive political and economic movement in the Western Hemisphere.

In the Pacific, the United States encouraged the development of the Asia Pacific Economic Cooperation (APEC) group for similar reasons. Like NAFTA or EAI, APEC should encourage regional integration, liberalization, and cooperation in the context of a global, outward orientation. All three structures should also encourage their members to recognize common interests and responsibilities. These new structures of engagement can help keep US political leaders and the US public involved abroad while assuring them that other nations will help bear the load.

Moreover, these economic structures can contribute to greater security cooperation. For example, strong United States–European Union ties are vital to a healthy NATO. (The Union is itself an example of employing economic integration to overcome historical animosities.) US-Japanese economic cooperation—through macroeconomic policies or microeconomic adjustments involving such ventures as the Structural Impediments Initiative (SII)—provides a more stable foundation for the US-Japan Security Treaty. The recent efforts of the Association of Southeast Asian Nations' (ASEAN) Post Ministerial Conference (PMC) to launch a regional security dialogue are supported by the attention ASEAN or APEC directs to the participants' mutual economic interests.

The United States has led the way in establishing this economic-security-political "architecture" with East Asia, Latin America, and Europe. Nevertheless, most observers, including those in the United States, have not detected the interrelationships among seemingly disparate policies toward various regions. Neither President Bush nor President Clinton explicitly laid out such a blueprint, although their policies have started its construction. So the American public has only seen piecemeal presentations of these efforts. This structure is new and fragile. The exact course of future US engagement remains uncertain. For these post–Cold War partnerships to take root, the United States' international compatriots will need to demonstrate their commitment to making the basic strategy work. At the most fundamental level, these potential partners must demonstrate that they will assume broader responsibilities and outlooks.

Korea at the Launch of the Post–Cold War World

In 1970 President Park Chung Hee captured the essence of Korean modernization in one short sentence: "In human life, economics precedes politics or culture." As Il SaKong points out in *Korea in the World Economy* (1993, 24–25), President Park's vision was focused but not too narrow. For Korea, economic development was the first step on a number of journeys: initially to meet basic human needs, then to develop democracy, to defend against a neighboring, totalitarian Sparta bent on destruction, and eventually even to unify the nation.

This strategy has molded the Korea that has entered the post–Cold War world. It undoubtedly launches Korea forward with certain advantages. As both SaKong and the authors of the World Bank's *The East Asian Miracle* highlight, the overriding purpose of the Korean economic engine has been to promote exports. Key components of the device are in excellent working order and capable of broader application. The Korean people, who have labored intensely to achieve so much, are highly educated and motivated. They are served by many skilled government technocrats. The government seems intent on, and capable of, maintaining the fundamentals of macroeconomic stability.

Building on these attributes, Korean manufacturing is making the transition both to higher value-added production and gradually to more diverse markets. To an increasing degree, Korean companies are moving toward globalized operations; there has been a parallel increase in Korea's outward foreign direct investment.

Pragmatic Korean economic management has also learned from past mistakes. For example, after government-led plans to build up heavy and chemical industries stumbled in the 1970s, Korea shifted toward more reliance on private initiative while also employing stabilization and structural reform policies to rectify imbalances. Similarly, President Kim Young Sam's government appears to have recognized that Korea's 40 years of economic success have created rigidities that could handicap the country's development in the post–Cold War era. Equally important, these habits could harm Korea's ties with the United States and others at a time when international relations are in flux. Therefore, the new Korean government is turning to a difficult but strategically sound agenda: deregulating tightly controlled financial markets, ordering real-name financial transactions while protecting confidentiality, attacking corruption, and promoting trade liberalization that should lead to more efficient resource allocation and help check market power.

These new policies are in Korea's self-interest. Repression of interest rates and credit allocation have outlived any usefulness they once may have had. Credit allocation is inefficient, creates distortions in the industrial structure, favors large conglomerates to the disadvantage of small and medium-sized entrepreneurs and businesses, leads to overleveraged balance sheets, and is a breeding ground for corruption.[3]

The strict controls on Korean financial markets are also limiting foreign investment. To an increasing degree, foreign direct investment will be especially important as a means of transmitting technology, production processes, and know-how. For many US companies, licensing alone has proved insufficient. Moreover, US and other foreign companies have many alternative opportunities in the more open economies throughout Asia and Latin America.

There may also be signs of trouble in Korea's industrial structure and labor relations. The government-led growth strategy has favored and protected the large conglomerates (*chaebols*), to the detriment of small and medium-sized enterprises. This is important because the small-business sector offers economies a valuable resiliency. It encourages innovation and

---

3. For good discussions of the need for financial reforms, see *Financial Times* (Survey), "Korean Financial Markets," 11 November 1993, 25–28, and Young (1994, 42–44).

entrepreneurs. Subcontractor networks offer flexibility that can keep costs lower.

Moreover, it appears that Korean workers, after a long period of accepting a smaller return from large national gains, have been insisting recently on wage boosts that outstrip productivity increases. To avoid pricing themselves out of the market, Korean firms will need investments, technology, and processes to attain labor productivity gains and shift toward a different product mix. I suspect Korea will also need a labor relations system that enables workers to feel like valuable contributors to, and beneficiaries of, business performance.[4]

The most dangerous by-product of Korea's efficient export engine is its mercantilist atmosphere, which the public has been inhaling for 40 years. First, there are the formal barriers to imports, which successive governments have slowly begun to dismantle. But the nontransparent restrictions could turn out to be even more troublesome. Officials have used customs rules and product standards to thwart importers. "Anti-import" campaigns have fueled strong sentiments against foreigners and their goods. Liberalization agreements have been criticized as bullying. Foreign trade officials are caricatured or even attacked in effigy. Korean officials who have tried to open markets are too frequently dismissed (for example, in 1990) to placate public opposition or for being wrong-headed; such dismissals have not encouraged their successors to challenge the old ways.

These mercantilist actions paint an international image of Korea that is, to be frank, terrible. The Korean public appears insular, even xenophobic, and hostile. The country does not present itself well in comparison with other East Asian, and now Latin, economies that have combined an export-push strategy with more open domestic markets. Perhaps Korea's geopolitical position and military standoff have contributed to its people's sense of insecurity and economic defensiveness. That response would be ironic, because the military threat should make Korea more sensitive to foreign, especially US, goodwill. Korea's resistance to imports and its grudging economic openness make it appear unwilling to assume a fair share of international obligations in a post–Cold War world.

In the realm of foreign policy, Korea has taken steps that could enable it to play a more constructive role. As President Park foresaw, Korea's economic vitality has given it leverage with its neighbors.

During 1991–92, Korea achieved UN membership and recognition by the People's Republic of China and the then–Soviet Union. Indeed, Korea has moved quickly to establish an economic, cultural, and academic presence in China. According to the *Washington Post*, Korea was already China's seventh largest trading partner late in 1993. About the same time, the Korean government was forecasting two-way trade with China at

---

4. See Noland (1990, 52) for discussion of the history of the labor market issue.

about $12 billion, making it Korea's third largest trade partner. The 3,000 Korean students studying in China ranked second only to the Japanese students there. And an influx of opera singers, fashion designers, and restaurant owners (and even four military attachés) are contributing to the push for a new Sino-Korean relationship ("South Korea Makes Inroads in China," *Washington Post*, 13 November 1993; Republic of Korea Washington Embassy Information Office: "Korea—Background Information," 93-31, 15 November 1993).

Russians also jumped at the opportunity to learn from the Korean economic model. Some Russians were interested in the precedent of government-led growth involving large enterprises. Others sought Korean expertise and capital in projects to tap the resources of Russia's eastern frontier on a large scale. Korea offered aid credits for this purpose. There also appears to be a growing and influential Korean economic presence in the central Asian nations of the former Soviet Union.

Korea has capitalized on the more frequent contacts it enjoys with ASEAN and Southeast Asia through its membership in the APEC Post Ministerial Conference. This is a significant development. For decades, Northeast and Southeast Asia were separate regions in terms of economics, diplomacy, and security. Now Korean direct investment, trade, and development interests are helping to draw the region together while securing Korea's place within it.

Moreover, Korea is moving in on the ground floor, as the communist states of Southeast Asia seek to emulate the market models of their neighbors. In May 1993, Korea signed trade and investment pacts with Vietnam, which should boost trade that the Korean government had reported as already growing from $90 million to $500 million between 1989 and 1992 (Republic of Korea Washington Embassy, "Korea—Background Information," 93-31, 15 November 1993).

These new networks should help Korea, and especially its public, recognize and assume larger roles and responsibilities. They could also help make Korea a more multifaceted partner for the United States. But they should not lead either country to turn a blind eye to the geopolitical reality, as well as the present threat, that Korea faces.

Korea remains a medium-sized country near the three regional powers of China, Japan, and Russia. All three have unresolved borders with one another. All three have a legacy of competition with one another, with Korea getting caught in the middle. All three have used force to dominate or occupy Korea.

A democratic Japan should be a potential partner of a democratic Korea, but historical tensions remain near the surface. A massive China is reawakening, although it is on the edge of a leadership transition with unknown consequences. The tension between economic freedom and the lack of political liberty in China remains a puzzle. Russia, in turn, is in the throes of a great transformation, and parts of its proud yet confused population may well turn to authoritarian or even imperial answers to their problems. Therefore, in the post–Cold War era, as in earlier periods, the United States remains the one power capable of playing a benign balancing role, which is very much in Korea's interest.

Furthermore, the sparks of conflict in East Asia can easily flare with other rogue powers, as Korea knows well. A former Australian defense minister explained to me that policy planning staffs in governments throughout Asia are now examining two critical security questions. First, they are deciding whether to shift their conventional forces from internal security to force projection. Second, they are asking whether they should develop weapons of mass destruction. In both cases, he concluded, the key variable in their calculations is whether the United States remains engaged in the security of the region.

Finally, the greatest challenge facing Korea as it considers its place in the region and the world may be to educate Korean public opinion. In an extremely short time in historical terms, Korea has undergone a metamorphosis from a semiagrarian society suffering ravages of war and the trauma of colonial rule into a middle-class democracy. Korea has made this great shift while living under the psychological threat of obliteration. Perhaps it is no wonder that the Korean public has not readily embraced the world. Yet Korea's future security and prosperity depend on a willingness of the Korean people to expand their country's outward economic orientation, encompassing both economic openness and cooperative security efforts. A strong US-Korean partnership, working at times through regional and global structures, is necessary to help Korea make this transition.

A US-Korean Agenda

Nuclear Weapons in North Korea

The issue with the greatest global implications for Korea and the United States is also the most dangerous topic the two countries face: the development of nuclear weapons by the Democratic People's Republic of Korea (DPRK, or North Korea).

The current major arms control challenge is the proliferation of weapons of mass destruction. The most probable security problems of this period are what US security analysts describe as "regional conflicts," as distinct from worldwide conflicts such as World War II or the Cold War. If these two perils are combined—a potential regional conflict involving weapons of mass destruction—the post–Cold War system will face its most alarming nightmare. The Korean peninsula faces this composite crisis.

North Korea's nuclear gambit is an extraordinary challenge for the Republic of Korea, as it tries to make a transition to a regional and global outlook. Many outside of Korea are anxious about this proliferation "test," which if failed could signal to other would-be nuclear powers (e.g., Iran, Iraq, and Libya) that international constraints are ineffective. Strategists also fear that the North Korean program could stimulate China to strengthen its capability, and the new circumstances might prompt Japan to decide it must have the means to deter nuclear threats. A few such moves on the geopolitical chessboard would dramatically destabilize current Asian security arrangements, with consequences that are currently subject to analysis in novels, not in think tanks.

For Korea, however, the implications of diplomatic moves and countermoves to check the DPRK nuclear program are much more local—and immediate. Koreans do not want to pay the catastrophic price of a failure in this early experiment in enforcing post–Cold War antiproliferation policies.

Without opening a full debate on this conundrum, it could be useful to identify some guiding principles for Korea and the United States. First, Korea and the United States must try to synchronize acts and statements. There has been a disquieting tendency for one side to suggest the other is being "too soft" or "too bold," with each partner at times reversing roles. If North Korea is going to receive a clear message, the United States and Korea must coordinate extremely closely.

Second, the United States and Korea should not muddy aims or intentions. North Korea needs to confront a clear, consistent message on what behavior is wrong, the costs it will pay if it persists, and the options for (and even benefits of) resolving the problem. Unfortunately, I fear President Clinton's pledge that "North Korea cannot be allowed to develop a nuclear bomb," is not an accurate description of US policy. The North Koreans have stretched US policy elasticity into a contorted result: circumscribed, one-time inspections will fail to achieve US aims while enabling the North Koreans to claim a "compromise" (even getting some benefits in exchange) and to divert attention from the key complaint. It appears, as one US official reported, that "the administration was huffing and puffing and backed down" (Krauthammer 1994). Alternatively, if the United States decides it has to "toughen" its response, it faces the dangerous prospect that North Korea will doubt American resolve and believe there are opportunities to circumvent demands through further pretenses.

Third, this experience demonstrates the importance of effective multilateral diplomacy for both Korea and the United States. If the two countries had a consistent message for North Korea, they would want it to resonate through the signals, and eventually actions, of China, Japan, Russia, and the United Nations. China and Japan, in particular, have economic leverage with North Korea that at a minimum could impose a high, ongoing cost for unacceptable behavior. China and Japan have reasons not to cooperate, and China and many others had to be pressed into backing the Gulf War coalition and the related UN process. But if the United States and

Korea determined that the North Korean nuclear threat was their highest priority (and if they conveyed a clear, consistent approach), there would be at least strong prospects for bringing other key players along.

These three principles remain valid as we consider policy toward North Korea.

Unification

Given North Korea's economic travails, its international isolation, and the uncertainties associated with the leadership transition in this communist monarchy, South Korea must prepare for unification contingencies, paying close attention to the three principles noted above.[5]

In particular, the United States could play a vital role as the catalyst for the "external" adjustment, as it did for the Germans. Unlike Germany, Korea would not be able to rely on the steadying reassurance of combining unification with integration in international structures, such as NATO and the European Union. Therefore, the United States would need to work closely with Japan—as ally, guarantor, and generator of ideas—to establish confidence in new arrangements. China and Russia would probably also recognize America's stabilizing role.

The internal economic, political, and social adjustments of Korean unification would be even more demanding than Germany's. A prudent *Nordpolitik* along the lines South Korea had been pursuing, with US backing, before North Korea clearly established its nuclear challenge would be a modest, yet beneficial, preparation. Opening basic relations with North Korea should not, however, devolve into the sustenance of an economic lifeline for a bankrupt regime. Korea should also consider cooperation with the United States to establish the best international framework for economic adjustment, with the help of the International Monetary Fund, the World Bank, the Asian Development Bank (ADB), and cooperation within GATT and APEC.

Relations with Japan

Koreans are understandably sensitive about deepening ties with Japan; they want to proceed at their own pace and on their own terms. Americans should respect this national will. At the same time, Korea and Japan have many topics of common interest—from security relations with the United States to China's development, North Korea's arms, and sound economic growth in the region. The United States has a security alliance with Korea

---

5. See Eberstadt (1993) for a particularly insightful piece on a country about which we still know amazingly little.

and Japan. Therefore, it would be useful to begin to strengthen the means for three-way communication about various policies. The Bush administration proposed policy planning talks among the three foreign ministries. Perhaps Canada could take part as well.

The United States might consider initiating economic talks—covering macro- and microeconomic topics—among the three NAFTA nations, Korea, and Japan. All five nations recognize that their common prosperity depends on continuing efforts to overcome barriers to openness; multilateral discussions might increase appreciation of the need to cooperate and may even ease domestic political opposition to doing so.

Indeed, if Korea seriously pursues its liberalization agenda, this development might help the United States open Japanese markets. Korea can argue that its actions call for complementary Japanese moves. Suitable Japanese responses may ease Korean fears that its liberalization will put it at a disadvantage. And US relations with both economies will be enhanced if it is not perceived as the lone agitator for more open markets.

Relations with China

Korea and the United States share a strong interest in China's development as a market economy that enjoys peaceful relations with its neighbors. We also hope that China's economic changes will increase its respect for human rights and prepare the way for political liberalization.

In a very short time, Korea seems to have initiated relationships across the spectrum with China, and China has been receptive. China's strong sense of history encourages ties to Korea, unlike China's ambivalence about Japan. China has pragmatically concluded that Korea has tools to offer, in contrast to its attitudes about Russia's limitations. Korea should recognize that its relationship with China has the potential for more than commercial gains; if fostered carefully, Korea can influence China's thinking, evaluation of interests, and policies.

Some topics on which Korea may wish to affect Chinese policies are obvious, such as North Korea. But other subjects of importance might not be immediately apparent to Koreans, who are still coming to grips with their potential to positively influence international affairs. For example, if Korea believes US engagement in East Asia and a sound Sino-US relationship are important for regional stability, then Korea might urge China to cooperate on human rights, antiproliferation policies, and trade. In the post–Cold War world, Korea will have more opportunities to consider actions that may not have a direct payoff but will strengthen regional and global regimes that benefit Korea as well as others.

Relations with Russia and the Central Asian Nations

Korea can also have an effect on Russia and the newly independent nations of Central Asia. Russia needs investments, particularly to develop its abundant natural resources. Russia also needs models of economic success to which its reformers can point. If some cities, regions, or business sectors can demonstrate accomplishment, they may even become the breeding ground of the next generation of political leaders, which Russia will need as it inexorably finds and then casts aside elected officials throughout what is likely to be a prolonged, turbulent period.

Some Russians have already tried to draw from Korea's development experience. Indeed, Korea may have particular influence on so-called "industrial centrists," who are attracted to Korea's support in the 1970s for heavy industry and government-led growth. Korea could be in a relatively unique position to influence the thinking of this important constituency in the newly pluralistic Russia. While Russian industrialists may not welcome the macroeconomic and other disciplines of the Korean model, it would be useful for Korea to engage them. Korea may also discover that resource development and other ventures in Russia can be profitable.

US-Korean cooperation on Russia is in the two countries' mutual interest. America is well-informed about Russian political and economic conditions and can share this information with Korea, as it has in the past. The United States is likely to remain at the center of interactions with Russia by the Group of Seven and international financial institutions. Korea can become a more significant contributor to these efforts in terms of insights, influence, capital, and aid.

Moreover, Korean entrepreneurs appear to be making a mark in Central Asian nations that are struggling to develop market economies. These new countries need international contacts with lands other than Russia. Such ties can help secure their independence. But America is distant. Western Europe has minimal interest. In contrast, Korea, China, and other Asian states offer both development models and practical contacts.

Asia Pacific Economic Cooperation

Korea and the United States have been committed participants in the APEC process from its origins in 1989. Indeed, Seoul hosted the third annual meeting in 1991 and as chair during that year played an important role in bringing China, Taiwan, and Hong Kong into APEC.

With the agreement to institutionalize APEC in 1992 and the 1993 Seattle summit, the organization is starting to gain attention. Now APEC must begin to produce near-term results while also charting a long-term course. Korea, an influential non-ASEAN Asian participant, is in a good position to urge progress in specific areas.

The recent report of the APEC Eminent Persons Group offers a variety of excellent suggestions. I group these in three categories. First, there are projects in which all APEC nations may take part. This agenda builds from the endeavors initiated through the 10 ongoing APEC working groups. For example, these efforts would include trade facilitation plans, human resources and training programs, tourism promotion, improved customs systems, mutual recognition of standards and testing, and the development of transportation and communications networks that foster flows of people, goods, capital, and information. This work could draw in other institutions—the World Bank, the Asian Development Bank, the International Finance Corporation—to help finance Pacific integration.

Second, like-minded groups of Pacific nations could build on the Uruguay Round (or help implement it) by pursuing further liberalization in specific sectors. For example, Korea and the United States could promote commitments by APEC nations to open markets for financial services and government procurement. They could support full enforcement of intellectual property rules. They could sponsor an investment code with commitments to national treatment, nondiscrimination, the right of establishment, limited and explicit exceptions, and a standstill leading to a rollback on performance requirements. And Korea, the United States, and others might seek agreement on competition policy rules and enforcement.

Third, APEC could foster subregional trade liberalization through broad-based agreements such as free trade agreements (FTAs). At a minimum, APEC should monitor existing arrangements—such as NAFTA, the ASEAN FTA, and the Australian–New Zealand economic zone—in order to press them to encourage trade with others. APEC might also sponsor subregional development projects or zones, perhaps including a North Asian effort involving Korea, the United States, China, Japan, and possibly Russia. More ambitiously, sub-Pacific free trade areas might explore liberalization with one another or with other nations, such as Korea. The United States should encourage free trade by being willing to explore additional FTAs (or connections to NAFTA) for nations committed to open markets.

In considering APEC's future, and even trans-Pacific ties with the United States, Korea should be cautious about the potentially divisive East Asian Economic Caucus. Malaysia appears to have launched the EAEC as an Asian counter to the European Union and NAFTA and out of frustration over the then-stalled Uruguay Round. While the specific purpose of EAEC has never been very clear, one aim apparently was to drain energy from APEC. Another was to promote an "Asia for Asians," in effect to add distance between the West and East Pacific rather than close it. It is hard to see how sending this signal to the United States would be in Korea's economic or security interest. At a time when the US public is reevaluating its global engagements, foreign lands that tell Yankees to go home may end up regretting the day their wish came true.

The ASEAN Post Ministerial Conference (PMC)

Korea and the United States are both ASEAN "dialogue partners," a group of a half dozen or so countries that includes many of the non-

ASEAN members of APEC. ASEAN invites these dialogue partners to an annual conference that follows ASEAN's foreign ministers' meeting.

Over the years, these ASEAN meetings and the conferences that build on them have evolved into a nascent regional security discussion. (Economic topics are also on the agenda.) For years, ASEAN's principal regional priority was Cambodia, but now its interests are broadening to include the Spratly Islands dispute (territorial claims related to oil reserves and sea lanes), the peaceful reintegration of Vietnam and Laos into a dynamic Southeast Asia, Burma, and even relations with China and Russia.

In an imprecise way, the ASEAN-PMC could turn out to be the political-security complement to APEC. Many of the same nations are involved. Given the central role of ASEAN, the topics of interest usually pertain to Southeast Asia. But as East Asia recognizes its greater interdependence, driven in significant part by China's revitalization and engagement, the ASEAN-PMC subject matter could gradually expand in scope. To varying degrees, other North Asian nations—Japan (a dialogue partner) and China and Russia (which have been invited by ASEAN for separate talks)—are already involved. Given Korea's increasing engagement in Asia, it should use the ASEAN-PMC to present its perspective. Over time, and working with the United States, Australia, and others, Korea might seek to heighten Asian interest in topics even closer to home, such as cooperation against proliferation.

As I noted in my discussion of US policy, the ASEAN-PMC and APEC could become post–Cold War structures that will support US engagement in East Asia. These groups represent the willingness of a new generation of outward-oriented partners to share the responsibility for addressing threats to the prosperity and security of the international system. The loose nature of these groups and their modest capabilities for concerted action make them better suited for encouraging constructive behavior than for bold responses to threats. Nevertheless, security cooperation may complement or support forward-deployed US military forces, which continue to provide the most important defense reassurance. In addition, when the United States must be the catalyst for decisive action, its ability to organize coalitions, even ad hoc ones, will be strengthened by its working relations with groups such as the ASEAN-PMC.

Therefore, Korea and the United States should look to the ASEAN-PMC, just as they look to APEC, as a structure for identifying issues of mutual concern, seeking to develop common approaches for dealing with them, and building a habit of cooperative action. This work can also help integrate Korea more deeply into Asian policymaking and maintain the Pacific engagement of Korea's fundamental ally, the United States.

Global Structures: UN, OECD, and the IFIs

Korea should also take part in international institutions with a scope beyond the Pacific. Korea has skills, resources, and experience of value to others. As other nations perceive that Korea is guided by more than self-interest alone, its influence will grow. This interaction can also help the Korean public broaden its outward orientation in the commercial sphere to other areas.

As a new member of the United Nations, the Republic of Korea should be alert to opportunities to contribute to a variety of multilateral activities: peacekeeping, humanitarian support, relief after natural disasters, development, refugees, and the environment and conservation, to name a few. In recent years, Korea has started to develop the institutional capabilities to help. In 1987, it created the Economic Development Cooperation Fund, as part of the Ministry of Finance, to offer bilateral financial support to developing nations. In 1991, the government established the Korea International Cooperation Agency (KOICA) under the foreign ministry to coordinate foreign aid such as grants, technical assistance, and training. Although the sums allocated to these programs are still relatively small, they point in the right direction (SaKong 1993, 146–50).

Korea should also become a member of the Organization for Economic Cooperation and Development. In the process, the United States and other OECD members should work with Korea to establish liberalization objectives that enable Korea to qualify. These requirements would probably look similar to those already targeted by President Kim Young Sam, so the twin agendas could reinforce one another. While Korea is working toward OECD membership, the OECD should encourage Korean officials to participate in various working groups so they better appreciate the norms and outlooks of the current members. Korea also can help the OECD as that organization struggles to assess the relationships among unemployment, technological change, competition, open markets, and structural rigidities; East Asian insights on growth should be welcome.

Similarly, Korea can play a useful role in the international financial institutions, such as the IMF, World Bank, and ADB. Indeed, it was encouraging that Korea agreed to contribute to the new European Bank for Reconstruction and Development. As a tremendous development success story, Korea's experience is instructive for developed and developing nations alike. Moreover, these associations will help Korea to continually reevaluate its own policies by giving Korea greater insights on global trends.

An Open and Outward-Oriented Korea

The special US-Korean partnership depends on the contributions of both sides. To an increasing degree, ties between the two will have to be founded on a multiplicity of private-sector relationships. Without this underlying network, the US and Korean governments could find it difficult to manage official relations.

Many American companies believe that it remains extraordinarily hard to do business in Korea. Anecdotes abound about licensing impediments, customs rules applied unfairly, protectionist standards, and blatant hostility to US goods. It is dangerous for Korea to lose the support of this constituency. Although American businesses complain about market access restrictions in China, one can observe that their interest in the market has been critical for rallying support for most-favored nation status with China.

American news stories also convey an impression that many young Koreans resent the United States, that it is blamed for "heavy-handed" actions to open Korea's markets and even for intra-Korean squabbles during its transition to democracy. This impression, whether correct or not, is also dangerous.

Korea and the United States share many strategic interests. There are many opportunities to work together for mutual benefit. There are also many dangers ahead if these countries drift apart, but this should not happen: the two nations are bound by a long, shared struggle and can draw on a rich combination of immigrant, religious, and educational ties.

Yet my vision of a Korean-US future depends on whether Korea's leaders—in and out of government—can persuade the Korean public to extend its outward orientation beyond trade to other matters and perspectives. The people of Korea need to form a more realistic, less insular impression about other nations and about the responsibilities it holds in common with them. The United States, for its part, should support and encourage this transition. But in the final analysis, it is up to the Koreans to make these decisions and carry them forward.

References

Eberstadt, Nicholas. 1993. *North Korea: Reform, Muddling Through, or Collapse?* The National Bureau of Asian Research Analysis Series 4, no. 3 (September).

Krauthammer, Charles. 1994. "Capitulation in Korea." *Washington Post*, Op-Ed, (7 January).

Nahm, Andrew C. 1988. *Korea: Tradition and Transformation—A History of the Korean People.* Elizabeth, NJ, and Seoul, Korea: Hollym.

Noland, Marcus. 1990. *Pacific Basin Developing Countries: Prospects for the Future.* Washington: Institute for International Economics.

SaKong, Il. 1993. *Korea in the World Economy.* Washington: Institute for International Economics.

World Bank. 1993. *The East Asian Economic Miracle.* Policy Research Report. Oxford: Oxford University Press.

Young, Soogil. 1994. "Korea's Financial Reform: Reshaping Society." *International Economic Insights* (January/February): 42–44.

APPENDIX

Remarks at the Inaugural Reception for the Korea–United States Twenty-First Century Council

WARREN CHRISTOPHER

No area of the world is more important for American interests than the Asia-Pacific region. Its dynamic economies and its growth rates make it a critical area for American exports and jobs. We have vital security interests and alliances in Asia, and we have an interest in promoting democratic values in a part of the world where democracy is on the move yet repressive regimes remain.

On his first trip overseas, President Clinton traveled to Asia in order to set forth his vision of a New Pacific Community. That community is built on three core elements: shared strength, shared prosperity, and a shared commitment to democratic values. Today, the United States and Korea hold those elements in common to a greater degree than ever before.

As President Clinton said in Seoul last summer, "Geography has placed our two nations far apart, but history has drawn us close together." In the 1950s, we fought side by side to turn back aggression. In the 1960s and 1970s, we began building strong commercial ties as Korean economic development accelerated. And in the last several years, as a result of the "second miracle on the Han"—Korea's democratic miracle—our bonds have become stronger than ever. Today, our two nations are linked by open societies and open markets. And we are woven together by 1 million Americans of Korean descent.

President Clinton and President Kim Young Sam have further strengthened the ties between our two nations. Each is committed to a bold program of reform. Each is committed to economic renewal. And I know

Secretary of State Warren Christopher delivered this address on 17 February 1994.

that President Clinton admires President Kim's personal courage and dedication to democracy. When President Clinton visited Korea last July, he made a special point of going to the National Assembly to honor Korea's vibrant democracy.

The principal purpose of the president's visit to Seoul was to address the security aspects of the New Pacific Community. As the president told the National Assembly, "We must always remember that security comes first." Today I want to reaffirm that the United States has a solemn and enduring commitment to South Korea's security. We are maintaining our forward-deployed troop presence as a guarantee of South Korea's security and as a linchpin of America's engagement in the region. We are participating in the new ASEAN Regional Security Forum as a mechanism to ease regional tensions and discourage arms races. And we are attaching a high priority to curbing the proliferation of weapons of mass destruction.

The United States is working hand-in-hand with the Republic of Korea and others in the region to deal with the urgent and complicated issue posed by the North Korean nuclear threat. Our shared goals are clear: we must ensure a nonnuclear Korean peninsula and a strong international nonproliferation regime. North Korea's failure to meet its obligations under the Nuclear Non-Proliferation Treaty is a challenge to peace and security on the peninsula as well as to the global nonproliferation regime.

Our determination to achieve these objectives is firm. Our preferred path is dialogue. I am pleased that on 15 February North Korea took the next necessary step and accepted the inspections required by the International Atomic Energy Agency (IAEA). Satisfactory completion of these inspections will help the IAEA reassure the international community that there has been no diversion from North Korea's nuclear facilities. It is a step toward solution of the nuclear issue, though very important questions remain to be resolved. I also want to make it clear that if we are to continue our dialogue with North Korea, it must resume North-South dialogue that looks to a nonnuclear peninsula.

The international community does not seek to isolate North Korea but to help it join the mainstream of the East Asian region. If North Korea abandons its nuclear weapons option, honors its international obligations, and takes other steps to conform to the norms of international behavior, the door is open for North Korea to improve relations with the rest of the world.

As the United States and Korea work together to strengthen security, we are also deepening cooperation on economic and trade issues. President Clinton and President Kim share a dynamic economic vision for our two nations and for the entire Asia-Pacific region. We are encouraged by President Kim's reform agenda and by his determination to open up the Korean economy.

Last July, Presidents Clinton and Kim launched the Dialogue for Economic Cooperation (DEC). This dialogue is a cooperative effort to stimulate bilateral investment and trade. The DEC channels US business views into President Kim's ambitious program of deregulation and liberalization. Similarly, it brings Korean business concerns to the attention of the US government. We hope that there will be tangible progress in a number of areas by the time the DEC concludes in June 1994.

The United States and Korea also are working closely through APEC to strengthen ties among the economies in the region. As the chair of APEC's Committee on Trade and Investment this year, Korea has a key role in efforts to liberalize regional trade and investment.

When Korea agreed in December to the eventual elimination of non-tariff barriers on rice and other agriculture imports, it helped pave the way for a successful conclusion of the Uruguay Round. We know the decision on rice liberalization was difficult. The resolve shown by the Kim administration demonstrates that as a great trading nation, Korea is willing to accept great responsibilities. Together, we must strengthen the liberal world trading system that has allowed our economies to grow and our people to prosper.

On the eve of the next century, our two democracies face the future in a spirit of cooperation and confidence. This Council can help shape that future to the benefit of both countries.

The US Economy and Trade Policy with Japan

LAURA D'ANDREA TYSON

On 17 February 1993, the president gave his first major speech before the Congress. He laid out fundamental objectives and a strategy for the economy to deal with the problems the economy then faced: the cyclical problems of a slow, jobless recovery from the 1990–91 recession. The economy was growing much more slowly in this recovery period then it had in other recovery periods. The economy also was struggling with a very low rate of job creation, also not characteristic of a recovery. In addition, there was the long-standing problem of the structural deficit. Our foreign trading partners were quite vocal on the need for the new administration to address this problem.

The president sought an approach that both dealt with the short-term recovery problem and got the deficit under sustainable control. The decision was to opt for a program emphasizing gradual deficit reduction, even though that was risky for an economy in a slow recovery. It was a balancing act, frankly—reducing the deficit enough to have a credible effect on financial markets but not so much as to impede economic growth. In the *Economic Report of the President*, we argued that the plan proposed was credible because we had laid out carefully what programs we would cut, what taxes we would raise, and what timetable the reductions would follow. In anticipation of credible deficit reduction, financial markets responded with a sustained decline in long-term interest rates. What that did for the US economy in the second half of 1993 was to boost all the

Laura D'Andrea Tyson chairs the US Council of Economic Advisers. She gave this address 18 February 1994.

interest-sensitive parts of spending: consumer durables, business spending on plant and equipment, and residential construction.

We have put the economy on a new path of gradually reducing the deficit relative to the size of the economy. The fiscal 1995 budget of $176 billion is about 2.5 percent of GDP, a substantial reduction from the 1992 figure of 4.9 percent.

The plan also reduces the debt relative to the size of the economy. Since 1981, the debt-to-GDP ratio had been rising, something on the order of 25 to 26 percent, reaching about 54 percent in 1994. Thereafter, it will gradually come down. We have turned the corner on the deficit and debt problems, and we have managed to do it in a way that allows the economy to continue to expand.

Our interpretation of the facts of 1993 and their consequences for the future is not just an interpretation unique to the administration. In recent comments, Alan Greenspan discussed the contribution of deficit reduction to reducing inflationary expectations and to easing long-term interests rates. He also said that all this puts the economy on a sounder basis for sustained economic expansion. Blue-chip forecasters and the Congressional Budget Office all foresee the same result. Sometimes when forecasters all foresee the same thing, they all turn out to be wrong. But right now, if you ask the average reader of US economic information about its prospects over 1993–94, there is considerable consensus that the economy will be growing in the range of 3 percent, that inflation will be in the range of 3 percent, that short-term interest rates may rise gradually—by perhaps 80 basis points over two years. So all the fundamentals for sustained expansion look to be in play.

President Clinton is a very energetic and active president, so while deficit reduction and management of cyclical expansion were important parts of his agenda, they were not the only parts. He is very committed to changing the composition of government spending toward more investment in the future. For about a decade, think tanks and independent groups in the United States have argued that if we were to bolster US competitiveness, we had to deal with the deficit, first and foremost. Then we had to think about how the government should spend money—less overall on the discretionary side and more on public investment, particularly on infrastructure, education and training, and research and development. The Clinton economic agenda does shift the composition of spending toward these public investment initiatives. We began to make progress in this area even with our first budget, for fiscal 1994, and we asked for increases in spending in all these areas. We are even more ambitious in fiscal 1995, in particular on education and training and on research and development.

On the education and training side, the administration believes that even if the economy expands and jobs are created, an active training and education policy is important to ensure that workers have the flexibility to move from job to job so that transitional problems are reduced. Training is also important to deal with the increasing gap between earnings at the top of the wage distribution—that is, earnings to college-educated workers—and earnings for lower skill levels and lower levels of educational attainment. The only way to deal with this problem is to train people better so that they are skilled enough and flexible enough to take high-wage jobs. A major new program we will introduce in 1994, the labor reemployment program, is designed to help workers find training.

The other important part of our investment agenda relates to research and development spending. One of the things I argued in my book *Who's Bashing Whom?* is that part of being a cautious activist, as I describe myself and also the president, is to figure out ways to support, maintain, and strengthen the high-technology base of the US economy. We have done that in the past through research and development support, primarily through defense channels. When the administration came into office, it was still the case that about 60 percent of US research dollars, which are substantial in magnitude, were going to the Department of Defense, the National Aeronautics and Space Administration, or the defense parts of the Department of Energy. We are trying to gradually shift toward more funding for civilian programs. We are mindful of the need to structure these programs so that they are not captured for narrow economic gain but that they instead truly maximize spillover benefits. We have introduced a new program, which the president and vice president have been very much engaged in, called the Technology Investment Program. It is a program of competitive bidding for defense contractors who wish to develop their technologies for civilian purposes. Moreover, the contractors themselves put up money, and projects are evaluated on their technical merits. Another example of what we are trying to do is a very small but successful program in the National Institute of Standards and Technology called the Advanced Technology Program. This, again, is a competitive program in which firms apply for support and put up some of the money. This program is slated for significant increases in funding.

Let me link all of this to trade policy in the following way. The administration looks at its panoply of economic activities as constituting a coherent strategy. One part of the strategy is to ensure that domestic economic policy measures will build a strong, competitive American economy. The foreign policy agenda on the economic side is very much motivated by a desire to secure more trade, not less trade; more competition, not less competition; and more global liberalization, not less global liberalization. Consequently, we have fought very hard for the successful conclusion and passage of the North American Free Trade Agreement (NAFTA) and for a completion of the Uruguay Round. Now we have to fight for its passage in Congress; this incidentally poses some important budgetary questions. Under current budget rules, the United States has to pay up front, and the administration must show how it will pay for forgone tariff revenues resulting from greater trade liberalization. We have a short-term budgetary problem, along with a general political fight, to make sure the Uruguay Round passes Congress, and we are committed to doing this. Our trade record on NAFTA and the Uruguay Round alone should dissipate concerns that this administration would be inward-looking, protectionist, and not involved in the international trading community.

That brings me to the issue of Japan. In addition to our commitment to NAFTA and the Uruguay Round, we have also been very committed to working with the Japanese through bilateral negotiations to deal with a series of issues, including macroeconomic concerns. That is, we have understood and continue to understand that the major part of the trade imbalance between the two nations and between Japan and the rest of the world is rooted in macroeconomic conditions. Therefore, an important part of our negotiating basket is macroeconomics. We felt the United States had delivered a credible and large deficit reduction program. We had done what we needed to do macroeconomically; Japan also needed to commit to macroeconomic changes to stimulate its economy and thereby generate greater demand for imports in Japan and help to solve the current account imbalance. This wasn't the only part of the agenda with Japan. Sectoral talks with Japan reflected several factors that have become widely recognized:

- There are real barriers to market access in Japan in a variety of sectors.

- Those barriers do matter to Japan's trading partners, including the United States.

- The nature of the barriers is such that they are not covered by current GATT rules and cannot be handled multilaterally.

- The only way to really deal with these barriers is on a sector-by-sector basis with Japan.

The complication has arisen primarily around one issue. In any area of discussion with Japan—be it auto parts, medical equipment, or insurance—the United States has insisted on measures, or indicators, of progress. We also were conscious of the fact that the same indicators would not apply in each case. Thus, we would negotiate with the Japanese about which indicators made the most sense in which markets. The Japanese initially agreed to that approach, which is spelled out in the framework agreement. The negotiations eventually broke down over the issue because the Japanese have maintained that the indicators are targets. We have maintained that the indicators are not targets; they are meant to evaluate success.

Why have we emphasized this? In much of the US policy community, in at least some of the US academic community, and throughout much of the

US business community, there is a sense that previous agreements have not yielded much substantive progress. They may have dealt with a particular process problem here or there, but after that, some other process problem has developed or something has changed to undermine the agreement and prevent results from being achieved. Consequently, US negotiations with Japan have lacked credibility; many doubt whether they have had an effect on trading relationships or market access in Japan. We felt strongly that we needed a credible approach, and we conveyed that to the Japanese. That was why we emphasized indicators. We believe that both sides would benefit from credible negotiations with credible results. We believe it would actually help to alleviate some of the distrust that has developed on both sides.

I devoted considerable time in my book to the case of Motorola and its efforts to sell cellular telephones in Japan. That particular case recently reached another decision point. It was not included in the framework negotiations because we were looking basically at new issues. Nonetheless, this case illustrates our approach toward the Japanese sectoral problem.

Throughout these negotiations, which ended in failure in early February 1994, the Japanese intermittently maintained that American firms don't try hard enough. That is particularly hard to accept in Motorola's case. The claim is not credible. The Japanese also say US firms don't make products of sufficiently high quality. Again, this is not a credible statement. Motorola invented cellular telephone technology; it is the global leader. The Japanese also sometimes say there aren't any real barriers to the Japanese market. Again, the Motorola case is instructive: when Motorola was finally given the right to compete in the particular Japanese market that it wished, the Japanese ministry assigned it a partner it did not want. That is not an example of a competitive, market-based opportunity. The Motorola case suggests that some of the general statements made by Japan in our negotiations really are not consistent with reality. Also, we never asked for indicators in this case. Instead, we had a decade-long dispute without real, significant progress. These experiences have led us to our present negotiating strategy.

I believe strongly that we have put the US economy on the right path—a sustainable, expansionary path. We have improved the fiscal soundness of the nation's finances. Certainly, there is more work to be done. But I also want to emphasize that one should not interpret the US-Japan talks incorrectly: the United States is committed to more trade and more competition. This is not about closing markets in the United States; it is about opening market opportunities in Japan. It is not about managed trade or quantitative targets. Every step of the way, the opening we seek is an opening for all of Japan's trading partners and not just for the United States.

Conference Participants

Young Mo Ahn
Korea Foundation

Ronald Aqua
United States-Japan Foundation

Eugene Atkinson
Goldman, Sachs

Lisa Barry
Boeing

Thomas Bayard
Institute for International Economics

C. Fred Bergsten
Institute for International Economics

David Brown
Department of State

Soon Sung Cho
National Assembly

Chang-Yoon Choi
Former Minister of Government
Administration

Ho-Cheol Choi
Korea Foundation

Inbom Choi
Korea Institute for International
Economic Policy

Warren Christopher
Secretary of State

Tong Soo Chung
Department of Commerce

Dai Chul Chyung
National Assembly

William Cline
Institute for International Economics

Richard Cooper
Harvard University

Rudiger Dornbusch
Massachusetts Institute of
Technology

George Eads
General Motors

John Eby
Ford Motor

Erin Endean
Hills & Company

Robert Fauver
National Economic
Council/National Security Council

Edward M. Graham
Institute for International Economics

R. Michael Gadbaw
General Electric

Tae Hyun Ha
Institute for Global Economics

Seung Soo Han
Embassy of Korea

Sung-Joo Han
Minister of Foreign Affairs

Young Soo Han
Ministry of Trade, Industry, and
Energy

Robert Herzstein
Sherman & Sterling

Peter Howell
Citibank

Edward Hoyt
Morgan Guaranty

Yong Hak Huh
J.P. Morgan

Vance Hyndman
Asia Foundation

Hong-Choo Hyun
Former Korean Ambassador to the
United States

Jae-Hyun Hyun
Tong Yang Group

Bong-Geun Jun
Office of the President

Robert Keatley
Wall Street Journal

Choong Soo Kim
Office of the President

Dae Joong Kim
Chosun Ilbo

David Kim
Korea Society

Hyun Chul Kim
The Sammi Group

Jin-Hyun Kim
Former Minister of Science and
Technology

Kihwan Kim
Korea National Committee for
Pacific Economic Cooperation

Kyung Won Kim
Former Ambassador to the United
States

Suk Won Kim
The Sangyong Business Group

Wan Soon Kim
Korea University

Yersu Kim
Seoul National University

Young Hie Kim
Joongang Ilbo

Pyong Hwoi Koo
Korea Foreign Trade Association

Lawrence Krause
University of California at San Diego

O-Kyu Kwon
Economic Planning Board

Hyung Koo Lee
Korea Development Bank

Jae Seung Lee
Hankook Ilbo

Kyung-Hoon Lee
Daewoo Corporation

James Lilley
American Enterprise Institute

Chang-Yuel Lim
Assistant Minister of Finance

Winston Lord
Department of State

Hyung Kyu Maeng
Seoul Broadcasting System

Marcus Noland
Council of Economic Advisers

Douglas Paal
Asia Pacific Policy Center

Chung-Soo Park
National Assembly

Ungsuh Kenneth Park
Samsung Petrochemical Company

Woong-Bae Rha
National Assembly

Sang-Woo Rhee
Presidential Commission on the 21st
Century Council

Lou Richman
Fortune Magazine

Hobart Rowen
Washington Post

Il SaKong
Institute for Global Economics

Jeffrey Schott
Institute for International Economics

Debbie Leilani Shon
Office of the US Trade Representative

Hak-Kyu Sohn
National Assembly

Chu-Whan Son
The Korea Foundation

Joseph Stiglitz
Council of Economic Advisers

Joun Yung Sun
Assistant Minister of Foreign Affairs

Bruce Stokes
National Journal

Daniel Tarullo
Department of State

Laura D'Andrea Tyson
Council of Economic Advisers

Richard Walker
University of South Carolina

Nick van Nelson
US-Korea Business Council

Jang-Hee Yoo
Korea Institute for International
Economic Policy

Soogil Young
Korea Transport Institute

Robert Zoellick
Federal National Mortgage
Association

Other Publications from the
Institute for International Economics

POLICY ANALYSES IN INTERNATIONAL ECONOMICS Series

1   The Lending Policies of the International Monetary Fund
John Williamson/*August 1982*
ISBN paper 0-88132-000-5   72 pp.

2   "Reciprocity": A New Approach to World Trade Policy?
William R. Cline/*September 1982*
ISBN paper 0-88132-001-3   41 pp.

3   Trade Policy in the 1980s
C. Fred Bergsten and William R. Cline/*November 1982*
(out of print)   ISBN paper 0-88132-002-1   84 pp.
Partially reproduced in the book *Trade Policy in the 1980s*.

4   International Debt and the Stability of the World Economy
William R. Cline/*September 1983*
ISBN paper 0-88132-010-2   134 pp.

5   The Exchange Rate System, Second Edition
John Williamson/*September 1983, rev. June 1985*
(out of print)   ISBN paper 0-88132-034-X   61 pp.

6   Economic Sanctions in Support of Foreign Policy Goals
Gary Clyde Hufbauer and Jeffrey J. Schott/*October 1983*
ISBN paper 0-88132-014-5   109 pp.

7   A New SDR Allocation?
John Williamson/*March 1984*
ISBN paper 0-88132-028-5   61 pp.

8   An International Standard for Monetary Stabilization
Ronald I. McKinnon/*March 1984*
ISBN paper 0-88132-018-8   108 pp.

9   The Yen/Dollar Agreement: Liberalizing Japanese Capital Markets
Jeffrey A. Frankel/*December 1984*
ISBN paper 0-88132-035-8   86 pp.

10 Bank Lending to Developing Countries: The Policy Alternatives
C. Fred Bergsten, William R. Cline, and John Williamson/*April 1985*
ISBN paper 0-88132-032-3   221 pp.

11 Trading for Growth: The Next Round of Trade Negotiations
Gary Clyde Hufbauer and Jeffrey J. Schott/*September 1985*
ISBN paper 0-88132-033-1   109 pp.

12 Financial Intermediation Beyond the Debt Crisis
Donald R. Lessard and John Williamson/*September 1985*
ISBN paper 0-88132-021-8   130 pp.

13 The United States-Japan Economic Problem
C. Fred Bergsten and William R. Cline/*October 1985, 2d ed. January 1987*
(out of print)   ISBN paper 0-88132-060-9   180 pp.

Estimating Equilibrium Exchange Rates
John Williamson, editor/*September 1994*
                        ISBN paper 0-88132-076-5   320 pp.

Managing the World Economy: Fifty Years After Bretton Woods
Peter B. Kenen, editor/*September 1994*
     ISBN paper 0-88132-212-1   448 pp.

Reciprocity and Retaliation in U.S. Trade Policy
Thomas O. Bayard and Kimberly Ann Elliott/*September 1994*
     ISBN paper 0-88132-084-6   528 pp.

The Uruguay Round: An Assessment
Jeffrey J. Schott, assisted by Johanna W. Buurman/*November 1994*
     ISBN paper 0-88132-206-7   240 pp.

Measuring the Costs of Protection in Japan
Yoko Sazanami, Shujiro Urata, and Hiroki Kawai/*January 1995*
     ISBN paper 0-88132-211-3   96 pp.

Foreign Direct Investment in the United States, Third Edition
Edward M. Graham and Paul R. Krugman/*January 1995*
     ISBN paper 0-88132-204-0   232 pp.

The Political Economy of Korea-United States Cooperation
C. Fred Bergsten and Il SaKong, editors/*February 1995*
     ISBN paper 0-88132-213-X   128 pp.

International Debt Reexamined
William R. Cline/*February 1995*
     ISBN paper 0-88132-083-8   560 pp.

SPECIAL REPORTS

1 Promoting World Recovery: A Statement on Global Economic Strategy
   by Twenty-six Economists from Fourteen Countries/*December 1982*
   (out of print)   ISBN paper 0-88132-013-7   45 pp.
2 Prospects for Adjustment in Argentina, Brazil, and Mexico:
   Responding to the Debt Crisis
   John Williamson, editor/*June 1983*
   (out of print)   ISBN paper 0-88132-016-1   71 pp.
3 Inflation and Indexation: Argentina, Brazil, and Israel
   John Williamson, editor/*March 1985*
     ISBN paper 0-88132-037-4   191 pp.
4 Global Economic Imbalances
   C. Fred Bergsten, editor/*March 1986*
     ISBN cloth 0-88132-038-2   126 pp.
     ISBN paper 0-88132-042-0   126 pp.
5 African Debt and Financing
   Carol Lancaster and John Williamson, editors/*May 1986*
   (out of print)   ISBN paper 0-88132-044-7   229 pp.
6 Resolving the Global Economic Crisis: After Wall Street
   Thirty-three Economists from Thirteen Countries/*December 1987*
     ISBN paper 0-88132-070-6   30 pp.
7 World Economic Problems
   Kimberly Ann Elliott and John Williamson, editors/*April 1988*
     ISBN paper 0-88132-055-2   298 pp.
   Reforming World Agricultural Trade
   Twenty-nine Professionals from Seventeen Countries/*1988*
     ISBN paper 0-88132-088-9   42 pp.

FORTHCOMING

The Globalization of Industry and National Governments
C. Fred Bergsten and Edward M. Graham

Trade, Jobs, and Income Distribution
William R. Cline

American Trade Politics, Third Edition
I. M. Destler

Environment in the New World Order
Daniel C. Esty

Regionalism and Globalism in the World Economic System
Jeffrey A. Frankel

Overseeing Global Capital Markets
Morris Goldstein and Peter Garber

Global Competition Policy
Edward M. Graham and J. David Richardson

Toward a Pacific Economic Community?
Gary Clyde Hufbauer and Jeffrey J. Schott

The Economics of Korean Unification
Marcus Noland

The Case for Trade: A Modern Reconsideration
J. David Richardson

The Future of the World Trading System
John Whalley, in collaboration with Colleen Hamilton

For orders outside the US and Canada please contact:
    Longman Group UK Ltd.
    PO Box 88
    Fourth Avenue
    Harlow, Essex CM 19 5SR
    UK

    Telephone Orders: 0279 623923
    Fax: 0279 453450
    Telex: 81259

Canadian customers can order from the Institute or from either:

RENOUF BOOKSTORE	LA LIBERTÉ
1294 Algoma Road	**3020 chemin Sainte-Foy**
Ottawa, Ontario K1B 3W8	**Quebec G1X 3V6**
Telephone: (613) 741-4333	**Telephone: (418) 658-3763**
Fax: (613) 741-5439	**Fax: (800) 567-5449**